G000117285

Bridge Beneath *the* Sky

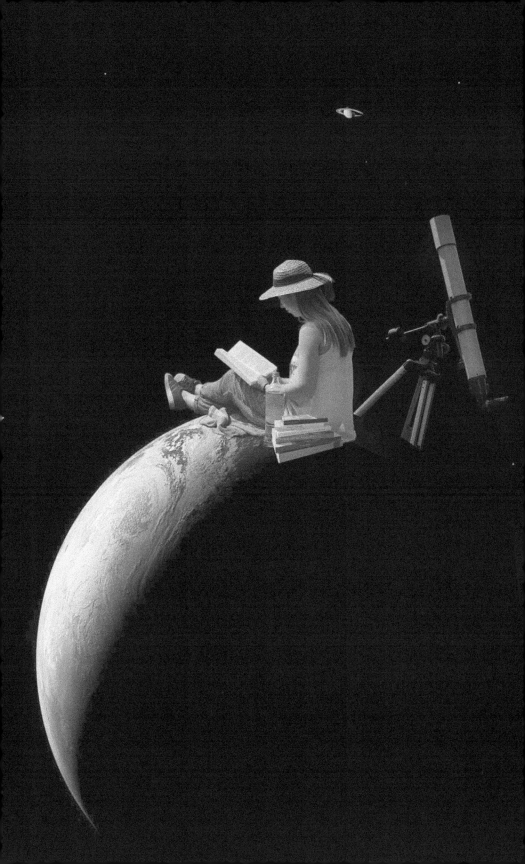

Bridge Beneath *the* Sky

Painting a Picture of a
Larger Reality

by

Robert Glen Smith

Bridge Beneath the Sky
Copyright © 2020 by Robert Glen Smith. All rights reserved.

No part of this book may be used or reproduced in any manner whatsoever without written permission, except in the case of brief quotations embodied in critical articles and reviews.

Printed in the United States of America

ISBN: 978-1-7358186-1-0

*For my lovely wife Kate,
without whom this book would
not have been possible.*

Table of Contents

Introduction

Why does the sun come up?

Is it the Greek god Apollo tearing his fiery chariot across the sky? Or is the sun a brilliant jewel set into the celestial sphere that rotates about the Earth? Imagine living your whole life without knowing what that thing is in the sky. Imagine one hundred billion people in human history, not knowing.

The mind makes up stories to explain the unknown. A group of people entertaining such notions can see them as facts. What causes disease? Is it unbalanced humors, as Hippocrates surmised? Time and again, plagues ravaged entire cities until even the monastery bells stopped tolling.

Why, God? Those who bore witness to the senseless suffering asked. *Why do you punish us so?* There were no easy explanations. Can we look to our mistaken assumptions of the past, and from them, create a model of predictability of what the big picture of our existence may actually be, if such a thing exists at all?

The gulf between science and spirituality seems vast at first glance. The methodologies differ, as do the conclusions. In simple terms, one challenges the other's preconceived notion of the individual or human species being at the center of existence, being largely incidental in the overall scheme of the universe, rather than given a privileged position by some divine or mystical providence.

I read Carl Sagan's *Cosmos*[1] as a teenager in high school. About the same time, I was also engaged in Jane Roberts's Seth books, such as *Seth Speaks: The Eternal Validity of the Soul.*[2] Both eloquently written, they each provided intriguing views of the big picture. Yet, they could not be more dissimilar. The former provided a historical backdrop to the development of science and the figures involved. It asserted the need for critical thinking and skepticism. The latter presented the idea that we exist in a spacious moment, and that one should listen to their "inner senses."

I understood how creative the mind could be, how easily it could find ways to trick itself. This is especially the case if the belief system was reinforced in groups or entire cultures. Fundamentalist religions tended to take a literal interpretation of sacred texts as factual, while other proponents of science denial incorporated unsubstantiated new age ideas or conspiracy-laden tales of government cover-ups. Both groups were evasive in acknowledging the everyday benefits and conveniences science provides. In the absence of critical thinking, the freeform nature of the spiritual mind has a great capacity to produce pseudoscience, in which every passing thought and fleeting perception that runs contrary to conventional knowledge seems to be given voice, regardless of its credibility.

Over the ensuing decades I came to openly present Sagan's viewpoint more, dismissing the potential for self-deception that seemed inherent in the psychological, partly solipsistic model presented by Roberts. After all, science had proven itself with clean water and electricity in every home. It had improved on the quality of our lives with medicines and telecommunications.

Still, something nagged at me intuitively. The general assumption the scientific community officially subscribed to, that the vast majority of people on Earth who believe in some kind of higher power are caught up in a mass delusion, felt inadequate. More than that, the ideas spirituality provided were something that science, by its very nature, could not, a sense of meaning, particularly in our suffering and sense of loss. Even if the purely material vision of life in this world were correct, it seemed unfair to expect the spiritualist to abandon this personal comfort. It seemed equally likely these spiritualists were putting symbols to something buried deep within their subconscious that otherwise defied explanation. Not that this explanation was in any way certain, but it was possible.

Over recent years of arguing with science deniers, I became aware of not just the dangers of pseudoscience, but also the prejudicial attitudes that existed among my science-advocating peers online. Not just toward religion, but any fringe or spiritually laced idea. Even philosophy itself, the underpinnings of scientific inquiry, was attacked, as I was told it was no longer useful in this age of rigorous experimentation.

Though hyperbolic reactions like these came as a bit of a shock, I understood the cauldron of frustration from which they came. A child of the eighties, I recalled vividly a new age movement that had firmly taken root in society. The crystal craze manifested in mall kiosks and display cases exhibiting necklaces set with differently colored shards of quartz. A seemingly endless variety of thumbnail-sized, glossy stones were held in bins. With the proficiency of a geologist, the storekeeper could explain the particular attributes each type of stone possessed for energy work. Rose quartz had the qualities of unconditional love; for amethyst, it was purification and shielding against negative energies. And there was absolutely no scientific basis whatsoever. There was no indication the salesperson knew of the processes through which the rock had been formed. They could make vague references to "energies," yet did not reveal how different frequencies of light interacted with the crystalline matrix to produce its unique appearance. People unquestioningly carried these things around in their pockets, hung them from rearview mirrors, as if collectively agreeing to a suspension of disbelief with the same regard as carrying a lucky rabbit's foot. This was evidently a matter of symbols that brought comfort and a sense of empowerment. But where do we draw the line between realism and a playful and imaginative adaptation? More importantly, why were belief systems that responsibly integrated both ways of viewing the world so scarce?

My own experience had been replete with highly unlikely coincidences, as if events were carefully crafted to keep me out of harm's way. Statistically, serendipity does occur, but these occurrences were of such a magnitude that even my skeptical-rational mind had to concede there was some mystical element in play. Not divinity per se, but a supernatural author that seems to know me, keeping my life to a particular theme. Some call this God, or angels. I am comfortable with a degree of ambiguity. If there exists the possibility of a personally-connected big picture, I would like to know it, but not at the expense of critical thinking. I accept the truth of reality, whatever it shall be. If the philosopher Epicurus is correct, then death should be no more daunting than the vastness of eternity that preceded my birth. But, as we will explore in later pages, there are other possibilities.

My intention in writing this book is twofold: to paint a hypothetical picture of a metaphysical system that would most likely be correct if any were to exist at all, based on its simplicity and self-consistency, and also to present this view alongside science as an overall framework for viewing the possibilities of the world and beyond. This spiritualistic framework is not mine alone, but gathered from various philosophies forwarded by others. The world could be characterized as a plethora of conflicting ideological beliefs that are all too often also at odds with science. It is hoped that the ideas promoted here might lay the seeds for some others to fashion a way of thinking that respects and accommodates both houses of thought, a conceptual Rosetta Stone to understanding what life is.

It is not my intention here to take sides or pit science and spirituality against one another. Any perceived attacks are meant in the best spirit of cooperation between ideas, impelled by an intense curiosity and unbridled honesty. Rather, this book deals with speculations on a larger context, a larger reality, if you will, that could conceivably accommodate, and even bridge the two houses of thought. If the reductionist view is correct, and spiritual beliefs can be summed up to a misunderstanding founded in a completely erroneous tendency toward human centrism, then surely a focus on education will eventually overcome. But if spirituality is instead an integral part of a bigger picture to who we are, maybe we owe it to ourselves to step back and ask if we could better frame the big questions. Like many others before me, postulating the rising sun, I want to comprehend the mystery of this thing called life. I want to know *why*.

ONE

Origins

When Once We Gazed Upon the Stars

Surely, one of our pre-sapient ancestors sought to climb the highest tree so that they could touch the moon.

No one is given an instruction manual when they are born on how to live their life. Certainly, some might try to fill the role of guide. More often than not, individuals will find themselves thrust into religious or cultural expectations. An older relative might impart a bit of wisdom compiled from their experience. Some seek out life's answers by learning about the world through academia, while, for others, education may be less accessible, due to cultural or financial reasons. Some make it a practice to travel, learning about the world's various belief systems firsthand.

Some societal expectations are universal to all cultures. We tend to get wiser as we age, for instance, and sometimes we become more cynical. People are encouraged to help those in need, family ties being the most obligating. Self-improvement and experience are both highly prized.

We learn in childhood that new people emerge into the world all the time, and that we will all someday die. Both constitute an element of mystery. For some, a finite existence is met with great trepidation, prompting a race against time to seek out enjoyment and make one's mark before the inevitable end. In contrast, spiritualists reassure themselves that the end is not so daunting, but a type of rebirth.

Several thousand years ago, agriculture assisted in the birth of sedentary civilization. Our understanding of the natural forces underpinning our place in the universe has grown exponentially in the last few centuries. And yet, the most fundamental questions remain:

Is there a God, or compelling force behind our existence? Is there a particular way we should live? Do we continue in some fashion beyond death?

Belief systems are mental constructs in the abstract landscape of ideas. These constructions are composed of concepts, such as people, deities, and nature, in different relationships to each other. Practically every possible configuration of belief system has been proposed, each with a compulsory set of ritual or meditative practices expected of followers. Objective evidence has never been produced by these means that make the case to skeptics, beyond any doubt, of a system superseding our own physical reality. This does not mean such a larger reality does not exist, only that none of these metaphysical frameworks is more valid than any other, as no human being has discovered definitive, reproducible evidence. In other words, there is no denomination or cult whose followers visibly take to the skies in unaided flight, perform public feats of telekinesis (moving objects with the mind), or open golden portals to a higher realm. Such abilities flaunted before television cameras and scientific inquiry would surely be evidence that something completely new had been discovered, though those individual's interpretation of what they had uncovered would still be in question.

In lieu of such a metaphysical Holy Grail, striking a tenuous balance between *the honesty of not knowing,* and *the reassurance of existence beyond life* might prove to be a valuable find in itself. This would involve using what we know for sure as a springboard for faith to take some recognizable shape that is consistent with the rest. It would require of us that we envision as large a picture as possible, while keeping imagination of particulars to a minimum. This context rests upon one assumption: that both houses of thought, the humble and unassuming inquisitiveness of science, and the surety of an unshaped faith, are equally valid.*

---

* "Validity" is used loosely here. In itself, extrapolating a larger aspect of existence would be an example of inductive reasoning, to which the term *cogency* would apply.

We are assemblages of molecular machines,[3] the universe made animated. If we consider human beings to be part of the universe, this fact is indisputable, though the conclusions drawn from it may vary.

Theologian William Paley's watchmaker analogy epitomizes what many spiritualists believe, that the universe is so finely tuned and functionally dynamic that it must be designed, thus, necessitating the existence of a designer. It naturally follows that this designer would have to yield enormous, if not infinite power and knowledge. Such an extraordinary being could conceivably light the Sun with minimal effort *and* hear the fall of every sparrow. The majority of religious practitioners are split into two camps: that God intervenes on human affairs (theism), or that God set the world into motion while remaining outside of it, letting it unfold from the blueprint nested within (deism). For example, the founding fathers of America were deists, believing America's emergence to be predestined, while prayer, eliciting God for help in matters of daily life, is an activity closely linked with theism.

The view of science is that no creator is necessary. Where design is perceived, it is we projecting our familiar human characteristics onto nonliving things. This anthropomorphism proves to be a conceptual box it is difficult to think outside of. And the most complex organization known to exist, the human body, was not created all at once. Just as timekeeping devices essentially evolved in steps from sundials into solid-state computerized hardware, there were many stages of development for life. Molecules jiggled and clicked into random configurations, perpetuated by energy in the form of lightning and ultraviolet light in tumultuous early Earth. Over time, some molecules were able to copy themselves and this was the spark of life. If a divine hand were at work, it would have been present in the spatial geometries and force strengths of matter, which is at least partly consistent with the deist view.

A common misconception is that scientists are almost always atheists, but in fact many scientists are religious. These individuals put their personal beliefs aside at work because they aren't relevant. Science is about measuring the physical world. By all regards, God is immeasurable, therefore science has no place there. Sir Isaac Newton was a devout, though wayward Catholic. Astronomer Johannes Kepler left seminary school to pursue an understanding of God's creation from the vantage point of science. A Dominican friar, Gregor Mendel is hailed as the forefather of genetics because of his work with pea plants.

Whether we emerged into the world from a designing hand, or none at all, it makes our presence no less magical. We knew little at first, as if awakening from a dream as countless generations passed. How to fend for ourselves, what plants were safe to eat, creating fire to ward off predators, following migrating herds, and the best ways to hunt, these things came in time, even as climates changed. Objects of the sky fell into a different category entirely. The Sun, Moon, clouds, and stars were in a realm apart from ours. They were seemingly eternal, remaining ageless. We could not touch them, but we came to learn they had power over our world. The heavens dictated the seasons and sometimes showed their wrath. We feared the booming thunder and lightning. Endowed with human characteristics, it was believed the spirits could be angered or appeased. If bad outcomes were not averted, regardless of proper offerings or worship, oftentimes it was deemed it was not being done correctly, hence these ritual practices evolved. The mind, it was reasoned, had a foot in both worlds. Like the animals, trees, streams, and rocks, humans had spirits too, not bound by the finality of death. How many times did an early human stray just beyond the safety of the communal campfire and gaze upon the starry night sky, mesmerized not just by the beauty, but its deep sense of mystery? Surely this surrounding shell of majesty was the greatest of all spirits. Surely, if our thoughts were pure enough, it could hear us.

Our sense of scale impedes us in our reasoning. The development of our neurology likely required only that we see in our mind's eye a mental map of the immediate environment at any one time for survival's sake, perhaps as far as the distant mountains on the horizon. Even when hamlets and villages replaced caves with the onset of agriculture, people rarely met anyone outside their own settlement in their lifetime. There was no reason to believe material reality was anything more than what the eyes told.

Imagine if we could tell our stargazer the truth of the world: that the Earth was not merely a rolling, changing landscape, but a great, spinning ball, and this gave the illusion of the heavens turning. The clouds themselves were water invisibly captured by the air, returning to the ground in rainstorms. Earth and the five wandering stars (planets) actually move around the Sun, which, combined with a respective tilt to our world, causes the seasons. The stars are faraway suns, our Sun, a very close star. Most of these other suns are too faint or far away to see, despite the fact that the night sky is permeated with them. And oh, yes, these other suns also have their own worlds. And the scales and distances we speak of are literally unimaginable.

Our stargazer might respond with outright disbelief, informing us that such matters lay in the purview of the spirits. Potential for analogies would be limited, as many fundamental concepts would have no easy representation in nature. But what they are indoctrinated to, familiar with, comes easily. The same applies to us, inhabitants of a distant time when science has determined much and the collective knowledge of the species lies at virtually everyone's fingertips. We're designed to see what the universe looks like from the inside, peering in through amazingly complex vehicles ultimately made of the same raw materials. The spiritualist still looks to the panorama of the night sky, perhaps unconsciously suspecting it does hear us, because it is our spirit as well.

Science and spirituality are two prominent houses of thought in human history that are known to disagree. Each implementing different approaches, it is especially evident with the rise of science denial in recent times that some form of accommodation must be reached. The rules of science cannot be changed. The scientific methodology that provided us with the modern world of benefits and conveniences must continue to work the way it always has in order to remain effective. But personal attitudes can change. Self-honesty can be practiced to determine what we know for sure, what we *believe* we know, and what is simply frivolous imaginings. By the same token, what is now met with criticism can be grudgingly accepted as possibility, however remote, if the belief system is presented in a way not discordant with a rational exploration of the human experience. *The world has demonstrated a need to believe there is something more to our existence,* and this is unlikely to change. In the interest of working together for the betterment of humankind, perhaps an accommodation can be reached through mutual understanding. In search of a conceptual framework that can incorporate both science and spirituality under one umbrella, it is necessary to establish some ground rules:

1. It cannot contradict what is known to science.

Everyday common sense isn't enough to learn about the inner workings of the world, but the practicality of scientific method is irreproachable. For instance, if a cannonball and egg were dropped from a great height, which would hit the ground first? Intuitively, we might initially suspect the cannonball because it's much heavier than the egg. Common sense dictates the heavier the object is, the faster it falls, an assertion taught by Aristotle. But it's not true. Except for cases where the air cushions the descent (such as a feather), objects fall at generally the same rate to the naked eye, regardless of weight. And it took over a thousand years for someone to test it. Most scientists in history spent their lives slaving over endless experiments, collecting data, often proving their own hypotheses wrong. It was tedious, and unless something interesting happened, often boring. It was anything but glamorous, usually with little reward or recognition.

It's because of nature's unexpected twists and turns around invisible corners that we can't just think about the universe and figure it out. Nature likes to trick us. Really, we trick ourselves, since as human beings we are limited in perception and understanding. Science began in Ancient Greece with the idea that repeating patterns in nature made it knowable.[4] The benefits and conveniences that separate our world from that of centuries past are products of this principle.

Technically speaking, all knowledge acquired by science is open to question, but thoroughly accepted fundamentals, such as gravity, inertia, the nature of light, and molecular and germ theories are shown to be correct countless times every day. With vast libraries filled with this knowledge, and comprehensive explanations of the methods through which these discoveries were made, it simply isn't likely that these fundamentals are wrong. In science, the word *theory* means the opposite of its common usage. That the Earth orbits the

Sun is a theory, but it is not questioned due to the enormous amount of corroborating evidence.

In addition, earlier, more substantiated theories act as supports for later ones. The layman position is that Einstein proved Newton wrong, but this is a misrepresentation. The curved spacetime of general relativity was simply built atop Newtonian physics. This clarification fine-tuned our understanding of measurements taken of celestial bodies, and, if anything, it was Newton's subjective impression of a clockwork universe that was challenged.

Overall, what makes scientific methodology exceptional is its brutal honesty. Experimental findings must be replicable, and are subject to peer review. Careers have been built on pointing out flaws in another scientist's claims. Once an idea or claim is shown to be false, it must be abandoned. These propensities, compounded with the fact that science has notably moved forward, transforming civilization in its wake, prove its ethical tenacity and effectiveness.

2. It must avoid over-structuring and the mutual exclusivity dilemma.

Religions of the world tend to share many of the same fundamentals, such as practicing acts of kindness and goodwill. This is a development stemming from sociability inherent in our species that allowed us to survive Paleolithic times. Also commonplace in religions is some ritual form of worship or meditation, or personal sacrifice, such as an abolishment of vices. Beyond these characteristics, the distinctions tend to stand out more than the similarities. For example, the Abrahamic depiction of a supreme being indicative of Judeo-Christian and Islamic worship differs tremendously from the multidimensional, many-limbed Shiva of polytheistic Hinduism, or the lack of an ultimate personality of divinity in Buddhism. Traits such as central figures, ritual practices, divine commands, and sacred texts cause divergence from a central spiritual theme, trading commonality in favor of distinctiveness.

More often than not, people will stick with religious beliefs that are familiar and comfortable, reflecting their social circles and upbringing. But in rarer instances, when seeking out unfamiliar belief systems and placing them comparatively side by side, one might be struck by the following line of reasoning: "They cannot all be right because of their differences. If one or more religions are wrong, why would any of them be right?" Following this line of thought, one might also wonder if they would just as fervently vouch for another religion had they been raised in a different culture.

If some choose to believe the Earth is 6000 years old as calculated by 17th century Archbishop James Ussher, directly contradicting geological evidence, or that sadhus* have traveled in trance state to the planets and given a different account than NASA's probes, the scientific community cannot take

---

* Sadhus are Hindu holy men, some of whom claim to leave their bodies and travel in astral form from trance states.

these claims seriously. But if spiritualists make different and sometimes contradictory claims, this works against the overall credibility of their claims even more than these examples. For this reason, not only must the accommodating spiritual belief system not contradict science, it must remain as unstructured as possible in order to do so. The framework remaining freeform is not meant to invite speculation about the myriad of possibilities, but rather, to focus on comfort with ambiguity.

3. Finally, it must be open to the possibility of being wrong.

This is the most challenging aspect, being in direct conflict with faith. Faith in God and continuation in some form beyond life are essential components of most religions. Though the evidentialist practitioner offers up teleological arguments as proofs, he or she must fall back on faith when opposition stonewalls those arguments from design. The fideist* relies solely on faith almost as a matter of principle, excluding the need for evidence. For some, faith and devotion are considered more important than good deeds, even vital to entering heaven. It's common for the religious to attend a local place of worship to rejuvenate their belief in the midst of like-minded people, but perhaps the greatest source of faith is drawn from personal experience. This is another point on which spirituality contrasts heavily with science. Subjective evidence cannot be easily replicated like the objective, independently verifiable variety.

---

* Fideist: literally meaning 'faith-ist'

No matter how impressive or life-changing these experiences are, it is difficult to relay this intensity to another.

People are simply uncomfortable with not knowing. Scientists have no choice but to accept ambiguity until experimental results point them in a particular direction, but ordinarily the brain is inclined to concoct stories to explain or support what it prefers to believe.

Philosopher Anthony Flew is credited with popularizing the concept *burden of proof* (perhaps best known for its use in legal jargon). For instance, if someone claims they are being haunted by the specter of their childhood cat, you would not have to take them at their word. If on the following day, that same friend insisted that God had visited them, proclaiming you should empty your bank account and join the cult they'd just started, you would have no obligation to do so. The burden of proof lies on them, and, if you were using good judgment, they probably would have a difficult time making their case. In philosopher Bertrand Russell's paper "Is There a God," he states:

> Many orthodox people speak as though it were the business of sceptics to disprove received dogmas rather than of dogmatists to prove them. This is, of course, a mistake. If I were to suggest that between the Earth and Mars there is a china teapot revolving about the sun in an elliptical orbit, nobody would be able to disprove my assertion provided I were careful to add

that the teapot is too small to be revealed even by our most powerful telescopes. But if I were to go on to say that, since my assertion cannot be disproved, it is intolerable presumption on the part of human reason to doubt it, I should rightly be thought to be talking nonsense. If, however, the existence of such a teapot were affirmed in ancient books, taught as the sacred truth every Sunday, and instilled into the minds of children at school, hesitation to believe in its existence would become a mark of eccentricity and entitle the doubter to the attentions of the psychiatrist in an enlightened age or of the Inquisitor in an earlier time.[5]

Were we talking about elements like afterlife and divine judgment common in religious beliefs, these doctrines would apply to all people. This arguably makes the burden of proof even more relevant, since it claims to speak for many, and not just the individual or group making the assertion. A religion promising paradise or damnation, the desired outcome being dependent on a particular form of worship, would involve non-believers in any case, at least in the minds of the believers. But there is another way of looking at it.

When a cat encounters a chessboard, it sees it as a mere obstruction to be walked across. Not recognizing form or function, the relation of the pieces to the board would be a bit of an *associative blur*, or blind spot, to the feline mind. It would be clueless to know how the pieces move. The information simply isn't available to its neurology.

Could it be that we humans are the pinnacle of neurological development, that there are no associative blurs left to us, especially in concept? Or is it conceivable that a larger system, greater facets of our existence, would present itself as a great associative blur? One that presents to the subconscious as an intuition, perhaps, that the religious assign symbols to in order to feel they better understand it? Paired with the sliding scale of relativism, it makes a bit of sense. If one were to put money on the table, they might feel more confident gambling in this direction, not reductionism.

One can debate this point by indicating that what we see in the material world, we usually understand, constituting an intellectual plateau of sorts. We imagine ourselves as living in a microcosm on a spherical world orbiting a star. To our credit, we were able to reason early in civilization that Earth was not merely the landscape we saw before us. We were able to *see*, in our minds, a much larger scope than features of terrain. Sailors in the ancient world noted that star patterns changed from north to south with a continuity that strongly suggested a globe. Even Ptolemy's geocentric notion of a universe featured this. To wonder if there is more to the story does not conflict with the nature of our world, it would simply constitute an addition. The physicality of our planet is not in question, but if this new context was something that could not be measured by modern-day techniques, this does not indicate its absence, only its evidentiary status.

If you were light, you could leap to the moon in a little over a second. In contrast, crossing our galaxy from one edge to the other would take over a thousand lifetimes. Think of each galaxy as a suspended, microscopic droplet of water vapor in a great fog slowly falling down a mountainside. Space is so vast that even light can take enormous time to cross it. And so, as we gaze into the night sky, we are viewing the past, like a consecutive series of photographs hurtling toward us at about 186,000 miles per second. If we look back far enough, we can see nearly back to the beginning. The bizarre fact is that through a trick of spacetime, the birth of the universe appears to surround us like some cosmic funhouse mirror.

It seems a bit shortsighted that some fundamentalists would think this was all for them, here on Earth. Taking a body of text written long ago as a divine communication might make sense on one level, a sort of instruction booklet from a divine creator. The most evident problem with this is trusting the authenticity of the mortal authors claiming to act as conduits. This is illustrated by the fact that so many figures throughout history claim this distinction for themselves. If the message were genuine, wouldn't it be consistent? There is also the assumption that God shares our intentions, wants, and reasoning. Maybe like parents watching their toddler figure out a puzzle, God would have us come to understand the rules on our own for the sake of our development. That's assuming there is a God as portrayed in Western religion. To view such a sacred text as a culmination of purpose in our unimaginably vast universe could be analogous to a moth entranced by a flame.

Though the defining characteristics of religions depict a prime example of how people are uncomfortable with ambiguity, we might also pause to acknowledge a preferred image of a higher power is one's right. Just as some keep a memento of a lost loved one, an urn of ashes or gravesite to visit, religious symbols and rituals provide elements to focus on. But contrary to the body of evidence principle, is there a way in which ambiguity can work in the other direction? We must acknowledge there are limits to our knowledge, and that potential knowledge lies in wait to be learned beyond that circle. By that same token, it seems shortsighted for the strong atheist to declare nothing exists beyond what we can currently measure. And by insisting the spiritualist give up the proposed larger context in favor of a more practical view, isn't the atheist really asking them to relinquish a sense of meaning to life? This brings us to ask what kind of people we collectively want to be.

Think of the mind as existing in subtle layers. For the sake of illustration, we can represent this with an upright funnel with a wide opening at the top, perhaps resembling a tornado. The conscious mind deals with the instant, the moment. This is

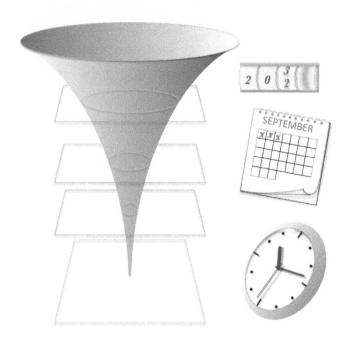

the point at the base of the funnel. As one moves up through these strata, larger fields of time open up as we think about our day, mentally shuffling chores and leisure time. We can think about the period of time that passes between New Years' celebrations, and how that measure seems to shrink as we age and time becomes more fleeting. There are larger spans of time we might address, relationships and career choices encompassing decades. We can ponder the entirety of life, overlapping images, sensations, and the emotions they evoke, wrapped in a sense of overall identity. The eventual perimeter at the top of this funnel represents the temporal boundary of life, birth and death. Logic follows that the longer we live, the more experience we accumulate, the more this funnel extends upward and outward, expanding away from the mere moment.

The mind works by deriving meaning by putting information into context. Context means grasping the circumstances surrounding a thing, sometimes even changing it from what you thought it was into something else entirely. One random word from a sentence would have a definition in itself, but could indicate any one of a great many possible lines of thought. One would be clueless trying to guess what idea was trying to be conveyed from that single word. Viewing the entire sentence puts the word into greater context, and so it is with the paragraph, chapter, etc. Each step outward adds depth to the meaning of the word within the surrounding outline of ideas.

We do this at various stages through the funnel of life. But then, thinking about life in its entirety, we reach the outermost region at the top, where what is beyond constitutes an unknown. How can we put our lives into context and derive meaning?

Spirituality is the mind's expectation of a larger context to life. Expanding on the illustration, it is the expectation of an ever-widening funnel, beyond what we can see or know through objective knowledge. Here, in this example, addressing eternity beyond our mortal existence is not merely a matter of before and after, it is a *larger* aspect of ourselves. In this illustration, we can challenge the naysayer asking for evidence. Can they provide evidence that this larger context the mind expects does not exist? After all, the mind is simply doing what it does, putting information into context.

In logic, this is called an *appeal to ignorance,* and is ordinarily frowned upon. But when we are speaking about a possibility as fundamental and all-pervasive as larger scales to our existence, it is arguably the prerogative of individuals to determine for themselves if this applies.

Where there is ultimately a lack of information, groups of people agree amongst themselves what must be there, choosing symbols from the environment (creating religion) to describe what might fill this larger space, this great unknown. We allow this perception of seemingly infinite scales to fill us, as when we look out to the ocean horizon, or lie beneath the stars, far from city lights. This spirit, many of us called gods, or God, but the space, this new context, can exist, regardless of the spirit.

Yes, there is a clear distinction between the material world and this presumed larger environment. This is the predilection of the naysayer, and it would be a valid point. As physical creatures, we have a clear bias toward the material, what we can see and feel. In science, it is all about what can be measured. For this larger context to be viable, it's necessary to challenge science's notion that consciousness cannot exist beyond a living, functioning brain.

One popular approach in science is that the universe is fundamentally made of information, which is non-physical, at least in part. The mind contains and processes staggering amounts of information. The big question is, does the information of the mind exist in the universe as we understand it? Or is it something entirely different? Science points out reductionist traits in the functioning of the brain said to produce consciousness, but a definitive answer to the question of information is not so cut and dry, and as a result, still lies in the purview of philosophy. The mind does have a discernible impact on the environment, reorganizing information, the stuff of the universe, into complex patterns nature would be hard-pressed to duplicate. And though still in early stages, the technology now exists to recreate a person's thoughts from fMRI scans, arguably bringing them into a material reality. Still, nature continues to surprise us, with its ingenuity, its compelling mysteries. Particles communicate back through time and even simultaneously across vast distances, feats that should be impossible in our commonsense view of reality. There appears to be a realm of activity outside of spacetime that we aren't neurologically hardwired to perceive consciously. If the flurry of electrochemical activity associated with the mind exists as part of the universal information picture, then could this larger field of activity also apply?

The information of the mind and its capacity to conceptualize and reason exceeds physics minutiae like spin, position, and momentum of particles making up the world by exponential leaps and bounds. Operating outside the confines of spacetime, a larger reality corresponding to the mind, identity, and consciousness would be extraordinary beyond measure.

If the mind is a part of the universal information picture, this opens the door for larger aspects of our existence. And if the mind exists apart from the universe, this certainly falls under the purview of metaphysical philosophy and spirituality. Either way, there may be sufficient cause for at least a hint of reasonable doubt in the mind of the skeptic.

From this point on, the question of a larger reality tethered to the individual will be referred to as a *conditional hypothetical.** The court of public opinion largely trusts in the scientific method because of the everyday products that are derived from it. However, this same method cannot address an untestable and unfalsifiable hypothesis. Even still, abstract ideas can be accepted intellectually without the need for experimental verification. For the skeptical mind to accept spirituality as a possibility that cannot be easily dismissed, the case for a larger reality must be compelling, and made at least as likely as an appeal to ignorance fallacy. It depends on the context.

The conditional hypothetical would be contingent on where the idea was being applied. To the world at large, it would remain a hypothetical. To the individual who already feels a connection to an unseen higher power, it would mean much more than that. If the case is made to the skeptic, changing their materialist viewpoint to one entertaining a larger reality in a new context, then the feasibility of heaven or the soul based on abstract reasoning has real merit, worth at least as much as faith.

---

* Though *conditional* is a term utilized in logic, its intended use here is less formal.

22

TWO

Windows on the Natural World

Are Science and Spirituality Compatible?

Someone who wishes to understand the world and their place within it might acquaint himself or herself with science, as this establishes guidelines for rational thought and skepticism, but also philosophy and different religions, constructing a well-rounded understanding of how people think. This is key to creating a steady, but pliable worldview.

In a manner of speaking, you have two brains. Though signals jump across the divide so quickly that they seem to work as one, the right and left hemispheres each have their own specialties. The left hemisphere leans toward linear processing, whereas the right brain operates with spatial constructs, dealing largely in matters of context. Neurologically speaking, there is pliability in this bi-fold representation, but the distinction is present.

Science is predominantly a left-brain occupation, dealing in precise measurements of the physical world; its language is mathematics. Understanding the laws of the natural world could be thought of as an extension of the deductive processes the left hemisphere is so adept at: science, an extension of reason. While the left knows how to speak, the right knows how to sing. Stroke victims who lose the ability to formulate speech typically can still carry words in the form of song. The right is the creative artist, the source of inspiration. The prevalent view in science is that the right hemisphere, artist and poet, aids the development of ideas by providing leaps of insight. But if science were the ultimate expression of fully developed left-brain potential, couldn't there be a corresponding field for the right hemisphere as well? Couldn't there be symmetry that reflected this potential?

Spirituality is rooted in the mind's expectation of the largest possible perspective: a context surrounding one's own life. Birth and death mark the periphery, beyond which there is no direct evidence of what lies beyond. In contrast to the scientific view of the big picture, spirituality tries to apply meaning, a place where the objectivity inherent in science is unable to go. By the same token, the spiritualist seeks a direct, personal connection with that larger existence, a mutual communication that lies outside of intellectual knowledge. Spirituality's sharply contrasting methods and conclusions with science makes it an excellent candidate for a field of activity corresponding to the right brain.

If acquiring a rational picture of the universe is assisted by right-brained insight, then it stands to reason that the critical thinking employed in science can help develop possible scenarios of a larger reality. Left can help right, as well as vice-versa. Whereas religions utilize symbolic rituals, an unshaped, *freeform faith element* expresses one idea: that we are more than we appear to be, even to ourselves.

Religions often contradict each other through mutual exclusivity, but a generalized, philosophy-based spirituality contradicts nothing where it takes nothing for granted. With each step, it is open to being wrong. But commonalities in religions have a better chance of being right in a larger reality than trivial details. Examples of these similarities include a higher consciousness, an existence beyond death, the enduring presence of a soul, and the persistence of goodness. Where we might hold a basic faith element in a larger existence with equal regard to an understanding of how the physical world works, maybe the particulars can be swept aside as window dressing while keeping the core concepts close to our hearts.

The cosmologist tends to see beauty in the cosmos, an endless canvas flowing with galaxies caught in the ebb and flow of unseen forces working in mathematical precision. The spiritualist has not the same tools, but tends to see an endless universe of light, perhaps like the universe in its infancy, the forces of nature having a psychological and emotional base. These are not necessarily mutually exclusive views. Indeed, if both sides of our brains can cooperate so easily to create an information picture of reality, are these two fields of viewing the world really that irreconcilable? While civilization is largely based in industry and technology, over 90% of the world claims belief in a higher power. What if the latter aren't delusional for entertaining the idea there is a larger force connected to their lives? What if it simply needs to be addressed in a larger context?

If spirituality is the complementary twin to science in a very real, neurological sense, perhaps we could think of these cerebral hemispheres as lenses in binoculars, or 3D movie glasses. Used together, what we see in multiple dimensions are not objects, but concepts embodying the true depths of our reality.

It is somewhat understandable why science steers clear of holistic interpretations. It is because of the track record. On numerous occasions, plagues ravaged Europe, leaving countless cities and towns nearly devoid of life. With no other explanation available, the senseless deaths of millions were attributed to the "will of God," punishment for misdeeds and original sin. Later, medical science nearly or completely eradicated most of such diseases in a comparatively short time. For millennia, humankind's history was replete with superstition, persecution, and belief in dark, malevolent forces. It should be noted that atrocities have been committed in the name of medical advancement as well, which is why a strong ethical obligations have developed alongside scientific practice. In hindsight, we were the malevolent beings.

The Earth was once held to be the center of the universe. Science takes an opposing view, that we are not the center, that in fact, there is no center in the larger scope. Science requires evidence derived from experimentation, results that can be repeated and shared with others, while the spiritual practitioner relies on faith, their evidence of the divine, personal experiences and witness of miracles that cannot be so easily shared or replicated. And while science maintains that matter forms consciousness, the spiritualist often claims the scenario is turned around, whether the material world is manifested by the mind of God, or to some extent by our own. On many levels, a hemispheric polarity of thought reflects the division in the brain. It's an important point to keep in mind.

One of the most remarkable acts in the history of science took place in Italy's Renaissance period. Astronomer and physicist Galileo Galilei ground his own set of lenses, improving on the Dutch invention of the spyglass, before turning it to the heavens. What he saw ran contrary to the teachings of the Catholic Church of the time. The celestial realm was said to be pristine and unblemished. But he saw that the moon was pocked with craters, rims textured by shadowing near its edge. Saturn possessed obscure features on either side, which Galileo referred to as "ears" (later determined to be rings as optics improved). Perhaps the most damning sight in the face of the church's teachings, however, were the four points of light near Jupiter. He documented their movements nightly, and it was clear these were orbiting satellites.* If these objects orbited a planet, he reasoned, then it was an instance of Earth not being at the center of the universe. At his own peril, Galileo tried to speak about what he had seen, but was met with opposition from the church.

If we could mentally fashion a pair of "big picture glasses" for those pious figures, they might also see the extreme opposite of traditional Catholicism of the time based in an unchanging message from an Almighty God. These figures could have employed critical thinking skills and adapted to the idea of change, approaching the claim in the spirit of discovery, with a curiosity about God's creation. Seeing the Galilean Moons with their own eyes, they could have even questioned their own beliefs, the veracity of scripture and

---

* On a good night, the Galilean moons can be seen through binoculars.

the presence of dark forces beyond simple human strife and outright rejection of knowledge.

These special glasses work on unraveling the core principles of both scientific methodology and spiritual tenets. When encountering a situation or idea, one can imagine how to process it more fully, from both angles. A mind trained in reductionism need only acknowledge the *possibility* of a larger reality, if they are provided reasonable enough arguments. Reasonable doubt in the purely materialist worldview is all that is required for a larger framework to work. That we exist within a larger reality can never be taken as fact, of course, at least no time in the foreseeable future. That's the deal we would make, embracing ambiguity for an easier, more honest conceptualization of something more to who we are. This includes a sense of greater meaning to life, without the mandates and sometimes unrealistic beliefs accompanying religion. The difference is a reverence for our ability to understand the world around us, tempered by professing our lack of knowledge. We need not clutter expectations of continued existence with too many symbols that obligate reinforcement of belief. Deep personal wishes and expectations, extensions of identity, these things are more fruitful than abstract symbolism created by organized religion, which often feel less personal.

To be clear, while the principles behind science and spirituality appear opposing, this is misleading. Both can be used to enact positive change or inflict harm. Both are about comprehending our place in the vast, cosmic arena, though the speculation beyond what we can extrapolate from observation must be kept on a very short leash.

Science and philosophy have common roots. Pre-Socratic philosophy dealt with questions about the universe, but also the soul. It would be an interesting time if science returned to the spirit of the pre-Socratics; keeping with the path of objective, verifiable knowledge, but at least entertaining a thin shell of contextual speculation surrounding it. That speculation could not be perfunctory, but would need to be grounded in a step-by-step logical process, never straying too far from the central theme of remaining *unstructured.* This means this fragile framework could not speculate very far without its resulting postulates being substantiated by meeting scientific evidential requirements. This makes the entire suggestion of such a framework sound infeasible, but, in fact, there *is* evidence something mystical underpins our reality. Half of the scientific community simply chooses to ignore it.

Parapsychologists have been studying psychic phenomena, or *psi,* with rigorous scientific standards for the better part of a century. It began with J.B. Rhine and his now famous Zener cards, bearing five individual symbols on each of their faces. Over the ensuing decades, these studies became more refined. The ganzfeld procedure required that the subjects' eyes be covered, and headphones providing a soft hissing sound be placed on their ears. This individual acted as the receiver. For a half-hour, a second subject in another room would stare at a picture and try to send that image mentally to the first. Directly afterwards, the first subject was presented with a series of four pictures and asked to choose the one the sender had been provided with. Many of these studies were performed, usually with some degree of success.

Some researchers were skeptical of the positive results. A statistical examination of combined studies, or *meta-analysis,* was conducted on these studies, showing an overall ten-percent rise over the number of successes there should be by chance, from 25 to 35 percent.[6] It's important to keep in mind that the more studies are included, the more consistent the bell curve representing these findings becomes. This is analogous to a series of independent coin-flip studies over decades' time in which tails comes up significantly more than heads, which is impossible according to our understanding of how statistics work.

Critics looked for any way in which the receiving subject could have been leaked subconscious clues. They also looked at the possibility of what is called the *file drawer effect,* a hypothetical number of unsuccessful and undocumented studies that would skew the results, then agreeing that the number of unreported studies required to do this were just unreasonably high.[7]

Precognition involves awareness concerning future events, while presentiment deals with feelings regarding them. Typically in these studies, a subject's physiological responses are carefully measured in the seconds before an image flashes on a computer screen. Some of these images elicited feelings of tranquility or horror, while in other cases, some of the images were meant to spark arousal. A meta-analysis of these studies showed a rate high above what would be expected by chance.[8]

Skeptics react to these findings with an attitude of casual indifference, as if the flaws in the experiments simply haven't been found yet. The reasoning is because psi is too strange for many to accept.[9] It's this preconception and others like it that a framework of contextual speculation would address.

Perhaps nothing demonstrates the dichotomy in our thought processes like the debate over free will. Physicist Max Plank wrote, "The assumption of an absolute determinism is the essential foundation of every scientific enquiry."[10] It makes a certain amount of sense that thought patterns in our minds unfurl from ones directly preceding them, in a predictable manner, and as reactions to external stimuli. Still, this question remains unresolved for many, even within the scientific community. People generally want to believe they are at least in control of how they react to events, if not having a hand in the formulation of the events themselves.

A research study headed by philosopher Eddy Nahmias of Georgia State University told a story to participants about a woman named Jill who had been fitted with a high-tech skullcap that could read her thoughts. Researchers continued, saying this equipment determined that her thoughts unfolded in a thoroughly predictive matter, in such a way that researchers could even accurately predict who she would vote for. But the entire story was fictional. Asked for their responses, the vast majority of participants determined Jill still had free will, despite the predictability of her thought patterns, as long as researchers didn't use the equipment to alter her thoughts. This persisted even when the results showed the predictability communicated a deterministic system.[11]

But how do we define free will? Certainly, it does not mean we have the power to do whatever we want, without physical constraints. For example, we cannot spread our arms and fly, no matter how much we convince ourselves we can. It's not within our power, no more than we can step into Ancient Rome by willing it. As far as action is concerned, we can consciously and deliberately affect our environment only through motor function (movement), including speech.

Another way of approaching the discordance of free will and determinism is an illustration: a collection of spheres with a figure at each of their centers. The boundaries of the spheres represent the point where the figure's internal, mental world meets the outer environment. In the first,

Representation of
Free Will

Representation of
Determinism

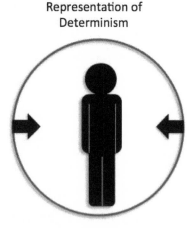

arrows point out and away from the sphere, indicating the figure's uncontested mastery over environment. In this completely centric view known as *solipsism*, there exists boundless free will, the capacity to experience anything the figure desires. We all know from personal experience that this is not correct, so we can disregard the model. The second sphere exhibits arrows pointing inward, toward the figure. This is the purely deterministic model: the outside world forcing itself on them while they operate under the illusion of choice in how they react. In this scenario, neurons fire in a predictable, albeit, complex pattern, their scripted dance only altering course by preprogrammed reaction with predetermined parts in the surrounding universe. Though this possibility cannot be discounted right away, it is difficult for many to accept. Also, as we prepare to put on our big picture glasses, one extreme existing entirely at the expense of the other seems like too pat an answer, considering how the subject matter is philosophical and open to individual interpretation rather than objective evidence. We are presented with two models: a free will model wherein the causality flows outward from the figure, and a deterministic model, in which the direction of causality flows inward, toward the figure. In one, the figure causes the effects in the outside world. In the other, the figure's state is purely an effect of outside causes.

The similarities in these first two models are the arrows of causality. From a perspective outside spacetime, the likely domicile of a larger reality, there is no cause and effect relationship, and therefore, the implied directions of the model would be simultaneous. We are using a spatial illustration to describe a temporal process, but it relays the idea adequately. This constitutes a third option we might call the porous system, a blending of the two aspects. This is not to be confused with moderation between two extremes. The free will model and determinism model exist simultaneously, without contradiction, even though it appears they should be in conflict. This absurdity hints at a principle that will be revisited again in later chapters.

As we don our special glasses and see the depth of the concept, it appears free will and determinism are perspective dependent. A great consciousness might look down upon the Earth and see stacks of molecules moving in generally predictable ways: buildings rising and falling, oil tankers and cargo container ships inching across oceans, foliage replenishing the atmosphere with oxygen, while stretches of cars on endless highways belch obnoxious hydrocarbon emissions. It's likely the surface of our world would resemble an ant colony to this higher consciousness, a model of deterministic factors playing out in symphony.

A single-celled paramecium would have a completely different perception of us. It does not understand complex concepts, or even simple ones, by our standards. It has no brain, no central nervous system to speak of. Some might argue it has the dimmest awareness of its immediate environment through the simplest chemical processes, but even this is suspect. The paramecium does not have the necessary tools to do very much, in fact. It barely exists at all. But had it the capacity to reason, it would regard we human beings as mammoth collections of trillions of specialized cells. In harsh contrast to the paramecium, we are able to manipulate our environment to a fantastically absurd degree, even in grasping the most incidental object. Our senses and brainpower allow us to collectively reshape the surface of the planet, or even glimpse nearly to the distant creation of the universe. Like great ships, we can travel boundless distances and are capable of wielding enormous power not found naturally on Earth. The scientific community rates the human being to be the most complex organization known to exist in the entire universe. And its use is absolutely free. Any cost incurred from billions of years of development does not fall to us. It's like hitting the cosmic lottery, a fortune we all tend to forget.

Make no mistake, there is no concrete universal baseline for measuring consciousness. On the sliding scale of relativism, we are the paramecium. But to this tiny creature, it would appear as if we could do anything we set our collective minds to, the paradigm of free will.

It is important to note a sense of scale is an intrinsic part of the concepts presented here. Nothing illustrates a contrast of scale more than the position of the Catholic Church centuries ago, that the Earth laid at the center of a very small universe,* while astronomical analogies do little to impress upon us the true scales of the solar system, much less, the universe. Our brains are designed for the savannah, and have developed little since.

There are a plethora of possibilities, but there is only one truth defining our reality. That being said, that truth may not be within our grasp, but may also be something we aren't thinking about in quite the right way. Maybe the question needs tweaking before we can uncover an answer everyone can accept. Moreover, in addressing the interplay between apparent design and anthropomorphism, perhaps the answer somehow incorporates both. Like free will or determinism, it can appear as either, depending on which angle you look at it from, and the mindset behind it. If consciousness is fundamental in quantum mechanics (the jury is out on

---

* The Catholic Church has since reversed their position.

that question), then, in the choice between proponents of intelligent design and evidentialist skeptics discounting the evidence, the debate may not be mere folly here on Earth, but a universal, dual-fold reality.

Is the universe designed? Or are we random assemblages of molecules in an uncaring universe? Perhaps it depends on whom is asking the question.

Here on Earth, a man at church or temple contemplates the unfathomable mind of God. Here on Earth, a woman sits in a lecture hall, breathless at the description of the vast cosmos.

Both would agree on one fundamental point: that the picture before us is much bigger than we are, more than what we know, and perhaps this could be the most fundamental assumption of all.

THREE

Big Blue Sky

The Environment of Mind

I remember when Magic Eye pictures were the latest trend. For a time you couldn't enter someone's house without seeing a book or magazine on a coffee table with the hidden images nested within.

"Just stare at it," I was told. "It will come." It took many separate attempts, but eventually it did. It was like peering into a new dimension of depth in the pages. But if someone had merely told me "cross your eyes slightly until your brain locks together images to the left and right, revealing the hidden pattern," it would have taken me just moments.

Our species stabs at metaphysical truth in a game of hit and miss. A practitioner of one of the world's many religions vouches for the authenticity of theirs over another. Some have more generalized views, placing their faith in energy work, or spirits from beyond. Some others simply profess belief in *something more*, a mystery met with both exhilaration and trepidation, but don't give it much thought beyond that. Then there are those who occupy their days with distraction from their irrevocable mortality, and the existential angst of not knowing what will happen at life's end. If there is a magic trick to understanding the depths of *who* and *where* we are in some metaphysical context, it likely hasn't been found yet.

We know from science that all but the lightest atoms that compose our bodies were created in the hearts of long-dead stars. We also know that we unfold from a biological template perpetuated through countless generations and variations. The pinnacle of nature's evolution is the brain, in particular, the extremely sophisticated human variety. No one was given an instruction booklet at birth on how to operate this device, though psychology and neuroscience has come a long way in understanding the mind and social behavior. Oftentimes, these resources of accumulated knowledge are neglected in favor of less diversified worldviews, with little perspective on history or science.

The mind is an essential tool in unraveling nature's inner workings, though it is prone to misconceptions. This is why a methodical process must temper imagination. For every mental wall that is raised, no matter how fancy or ornamental it appears, it blinds us to a sometimes ugly truth: that the world can be less interesting than our imaginings, even ordinary. That is why we must be vigilant, approaching the enigmatic truth of our existence with moral courage. That is why we must be open to being wrong about the big picture, from either side of the tracks. It is the only way for science and spirituality to meet halfway.

As creatures of the Earth, we are enamored by the same vistas our ancestors gazed at with a sense of wonder. The imperceptible depth of the blue sky lies rich with hidden stars, as if keeping a secret, only to be peeled away at dusk.

A light particle can bounce around chaotically inside the sun for a million years before escaping the surface and arriving at Earth several minutes later. The sky appears blue because short wavelengths of that range are scattered more than other colors. Whereas a tree's leaves absorb red and blue photons, one particular light particle is reflected by chlorophyll's chemical composition because its energy falls into the green part of the spectrum. Then striking the retina at the back of the eye, the energy is translated into electrochemical signals that quickly travel to visual centers at the back of the brain.

The brain's whirling patterns of electromagnetic activity range from subtle whispers to cracks of lightning, rejecting or accepting extrapolated information on the basis of sometimes fallacious abstract reasoning. When we think of seeing the outside world, we often imagine the light passing through the windows of the eyes and projecting onto a screen in the brain. Nothing could be further from the truth. In actuality, the world picture before us is pasted together from bits and pieces, a horizontal line here, a contour there, colors, form and function knitted into a situational awareness of where we are and what objects around us do. It is not a one-to-one correspondence, but an orchestra of carefully choreographed signals. The visual centers of the brain generally use the same neural processes we use to reminisce days past, or juggle a complex idea. In other words, the environment we *actually see,* as it appears in our heads, is made of thought. Moreover, it is processed through our memories and identities, making the depth of what we interpret unique from anyone else. Our background thoughts and emotional state frame each sunset. No one sees precisely the same one. This idea of subjective personalization, or *qualia,* remains an unresolved subject of debate in philosophical circles.

There is unquestionably an outside world in which other people view a very similar reality from different locations. In this collective reality, the locations and attributes of objects are agreed upon. On one hand, it is a series of approximations between individuals; on the other, it is a world we can only know visually by the limited information that shines through our tiny optical windows. In this latter view, the surrounding material universe is shrouded in a veil preceding our translation from photon to chemical metaphor in the language of neurons. The mind creates the sensation of light, arguably an internalized, subjective experience. We cannot see the world "out there" except via this chemical conversion.

Things happen without our knowledge and we see the effects later on. We don't need to see the rain forming in the sky above to feel it on our heads moments later. We accept that our view is limited and create a mental map of what lies beyond.

Stereovision gives a sense of three-dimensional experience and distance in space. Had our species sported only one eye, we would still conceptualize three dimensions. We would know some objects are closer than others, and that walking around an object would change its face, but it would be in concept only. We would not experience it as vividly as we do with two eyes. After the brain neurologically cuts and pastes the visual world before us, the final product could be thought of as a display. In concert with corresponding areas in the brain, the simultaneous left and right fields of each eye act as two overlaid displays. Equipped with fine pixel quality and enormous processing power, they provide a realistic depiction of depth in a constantly changing environment. Any lapses are cleverly filled in, such that we rarely glimpse so much as a squiggle out of the corner of the mind's eye.

Perception of the outside world is a neurological reconstruction. In the mind's eye, clouds on a distant horizon or looming overhead are precisely the same distance away as your hand: no distance at all. One could argue, "But I can touch my hand and not the sky." But their arm and hand are part of the reconstruction, which follows the rules and expectations of three-dimensional reality. The distances of the images in the brain are not applicable to the actual environment. They lie within an interior space. In a home or workplace, an individual is surrounded by the world outside, a shared reality. Indeed, thinking this way and sharing landmarks is how we function as a society. Someone has an educated guess based on memory and recent evidence of how the landscape beyond the immediate view appears. But behind the image in their mental reconstruction, what is beyond those walls where vision is obstructed?

Of course, one could argue that what is behind the images in the mental reconstruction is a nonsensical question, precisely because there are no distances involved. It could also be said that the visual cortex lies amidst a network of neurological activity. What lies beyond those walls, as an interior perception, is the mind. It surrounds that person completely, a mental universe in its own right. That being said, we know the purely solipsistic view is *not* correct, and the causal nature of the reconstruction's connection to the outside world appears to work only in one direction. Recall the arrows in the previous chapter, and how they determined the flow of causality between the inner recreation and the exterior world. A glitch in how things appear to one, such as a hallucination, does not affect the actual reality as experienced by others.

Seventeen-century philosopher and mathematician Rene Descartes argued philosophically that he could never trust his senses fully, for they could deceive him through trickery.[12] With his famous adage, "I think, therefore I am," he meant that due to the possibility of an illusionary world, the knowledge that he is a thinking being is all he could really be sure of. We have come a long way in understanding the world since then, but this questioning of reality remains true. Science has assembled a framework of predictability in observing the natural world. It has enabled us to understand how the brain functions down to the action potential of the neuron. We know what regions are associated with consciousness, but still not what it actually is, or how it connects us to the outside world.

Contrary to popular dogma in metaphysical circles, quantum mechanics does *not* mean the mind influences reality. *Quanta* are energy in the form of discrete packets, rather than smooth and continuous. Energy, such as light or heat, can take the form of either a particle aspect, or quantum, or it can behave as wave. In the double-slit experiment, a flood of light particles move through two narrow slits, interfere with each other, and project an interference pattern onto a screen beyond. It is like tossing stones into a pond; the ripples overlap. This interference is because particles are interacting in a wavelike nature. If the experiment only allows one particle through at a time, it will create the same interference patterns as before, even though our commonsense notions would expect this to require two particles. It is as if the single particle goes through both slits at the same time. This overlap of two simultaneous paths, or states, is called *superpositioning*.

When we look closely to see how the particle accomplishes the feat of being in two places in order to create the interference pattern, it doesn't produce the interference pattern at all. This is often construed as conscious intervention creating a particular outcome, but it is, in fact, the photon that is bounced off that particle into a tiny camera, revealing its location, which disturbs the system. The photon acts as the measurement, and in some respect, the observer. The outcome is not determined until a measurement is made by an observer.

Does this relegate our conscious observation to a mere afterthought? Not necessarily. Edwin Schrödinger's famous thought experiment involves a subatomic coin-flip determining the state of a macroscopic system. A box is equipped with a Geiger counter carefully measuring a radioactive isotope, which has a fifty percent chance of decaying within a certain time period (thus, the subatomic coin flip). If the decay particle is detected, a mechanism breaks a flask of hydrocyanic acid, filling the compartment with toxic gas. Schrödinger later added a cat to the hypothetical scenario (and apologized for it). The final result is a state of superposition in which the cat is both alive and dead until we open the box, thus making a measurement and collapsing the cat's fate out of ambiguity.[13] Though no experiment of this scale has been performed, much smaller *Schrödinger's cat states* have been created in laboratories.[14] It should be stressed that models of interpretation assert that although a state is collapsed from superposition to a single outcome, the observer does not choose that outcome, *even if consciousness is integral to the process.* The question of the role consciousness plays in quantum mechanics remains a hot topic of debate.

Another often-misrepresented topic that bears mentioning is holography. Memory is said to be holographic, possessing no precise location in the brain. In theory, any neuron has the capacity to hold links to any memory via some rudimentary, free-association "software." Any brain cell can contain the memory of a childhood toy, smell of a neighborhood barbecue, or the touch of a romantic encounter.

In holography, a laser is bounced off an object. Where that laser meets another laser, a piece of holographic film is placed and the 3D image is recorded. The intriguing thing about the holographic principle, and the reason for its popularity as a catch phrase in metaphysical circles, is its approach to space with respect to scale. Shine a laser through the film and the image reemerges. But this works with even the tiniest portion of the film snipped away, because it contains the blueprint of the entire object, though with less clarity. Each part contains the whole.

In terms of the mind, it means every thought has a potential link to any other thought through association. In cosmic terms, if applied to the physical world we know, then not only is a blueprint of all creation nested inside of us, but we each carry a little bit of divinity. Derived in part from Eastern mysticism, the notion of a whole and parts relationship is the cornerstone of New Age beliefs. Holography existing as an immanent, or all-pervasive, universal principle doesn't fall under the purview of science. In a diluted form, however, it is consistent with the idea promoted by the proposed generic framework of a larger reality: mind and identity linked to far more comprehensive versions of themselves within an equally expansive environment. In this hypothetical scenario, both interior and exterior worlds are upgraded to comparatively enormous scales.

The mind is already more than we are consciously aware of on an everyday basis. There exist deep substrata of activity beneath the conscious mind. One of the first researchers to take a profound interest in the subject, psychoanalyst Sigmund Freud, stated, "Until you make the unconscious conscious, it will direct your life and you will call it fate,"[15] essentially meaning that the majority of our choices and behaviors stem from there. Studies spearheaded by neurophysiologists Benjamin Libet and Bertram Feinstein showed the intent to initiate action formed in the brain up to seven seconds before the subject was even aware of it.[16] Not only did these results shine a light on a previously hidden feature of the human decision-making process, they also cast doubt on the notion of free will. Though his conclusions of determinism have been challenged, the action delay has been verified in experiments since.[17]

The aforementioned funnel illustration opens up as it expands to encompass more of psychological time. As the base of the funnel represents the fleeting handful of seconds one experiences as "now," an upward direction along the vertical axis of the funnel would correspond to progressively deeper strata of the subconscious mind. Moments and hours of the near past, and future ones anticipated, could be found here. Beyond this are still larger scales of time, events of the distant past and plans stretching years into the future.

Following this pattern upward and outward along its projected course, the gradients of the subconscious reach past the limit set by mortality, the perimeter of birth and death surrounding one's life, entering into unknown realms. This hypothetical model suggests that the deep subconscious ventures into the larger context, assuming such a context exists. In that case, would we still call it mind, or something else entirely?

The soul is an old idea, rejected by most modern-day philosophers. The notion that a non-physical entity is somehow pinned to, and motivates the body violates certain physical laws (like conservation of energy). Still, many experience that ineffable feeling that they are more than they appear to be, even to themselves. In this case, what cannot be shown scientifically is often taken as intuitive knowledge. But perhaps it's a matter of context. After all, a non-physical entity attached to the body still sounds like a description of something within the physical environment, which is not so ethereal after all. If so, how might this appear to us, in concept, at least? As our technology increases, our analogies improve, possibly becoming better approximations of greater truths, or folly, depending on one's initial position.

When watching television, there is, of course, a vast reality beyond the simple projection on the screen, the people, their roles and dramas. We can pretend, become engrossed in a program, but in truth, it is a complicated chain of events and processes that allows us the experience of watching it. The televised images of characters, cars, buildings, animals, and sunsets are not their true nature. Those things have a deeper reality. What an LCD device actually portrays, for example, are millions of shutters that allow a metered amount of white light through, while filters determine the color.

But it is not simply random noise that comes through. The device undergoes complex tasks to translate a signal, usually from a distant location.* These prerecorded images are at some point acquired from a soundstage where actors play out their roles in front of cameras. They are not truly the characters portrayed, but pretend for the sake of the drama and their own individual needs. Otherwise, they live a different existence than the roles they play. The many factors that contribute to the fictional portrayal we see on the screen are behind the scenes, and largely considered irrelevant to the story itself. When approaching a friend about the surprising lack of realism in a reality show, for instance, the scripts and plot devices that are obviously involved, they might retort, "Quiet, I'm watching my show!" Sometimes we're not interested in the backstage production or how the TV works. We just want

---

* The brain's further interpretation of those signals is another story in itself.

to pretend along, like an unspoken agreement with everyone involved.

The inner workings of the universe are still a bit of a mystery, especially in our perception of it. Time and time again, nature surprises us with its ingenuity. Interstellar gas coalesces into stars, igniting fusion, allowing life to develop on nearby worlds. Microtubules within cells, once thought to be mere structural supports, appear to perform quantum computations. A species of treehopper insect bears functional, interlocking gears on its legs before it learns to synchronize its jumps. The universe itself is so finely tuned in its forces that even a tiny deviation would cause everything to fly apart. The more history goes by, the faster these discoveries are made. The more we learn, the more questions arise. One need not believe in anthropic principles or divinity to expect nature's surprises to continue to unfold far beyond what we can foresee. It's a matter of predictability.

The root assumption of this proposed spiritual framework, that we are each more than we appear to be, suggests that each individual is part of a greater mind they can call their own, like the child who has grown to adulthood. Making an analogy with the televised, fictional program, this larger personality would be the actor, producer, writer, and director, any role involved with the creation of the program. They would use apparatuses and systems already in place to project this performance into the world, just as various stages of technology convey television programs to the viewer.

With such profound speculations on such an unknown, all we could really be sure of is that the individual's larger personality would have a much broader identity and presence in an environment that dwarfs the physical reality we know. It would probably feel more familiar to that person than the everyday life they live.

To the religious practitioner, this deep familiarity on a personal level may be virtually indistinguishable from the concept of an all-powerful being. This *larger personality* could be construed as a sort of local deity figure, an intermediary between Heaven and Earth, something that knows us and understands the depths of our despair. It is like a mentor that sees the unfurled life from afar and in its entirety, nudging us unconsciously in particular directions for reasons we cannot grasp, except in retrospect. It is like a lover in which we see ultimate, breathtaking beauty that at times feels like only we can appreciate. Perceiving a higher power through lenses of our personality and experience, we cannot help but mask it to some extent in our own image.

That is, *if* the larger context is real to begin with. Admitting it might be the fancy of our imaginations is the deal we make, but it's honest, which is more powerful than all the compulsory belief in the world.

FOUR

Seeing the Cosmic Forest for the Trees

The Question of Consciousness

No one is enlightened. There is no "one true path."
Transcendence comes from life experience.
This is something we all share.

Our information picture of the outside world is instantly referenced with memories, providing situational awareness and a sense of continuity. Together, these elements form a reconstruction of reality, and embedded within this is our identity, our sense of self. This neurological reconstruction is not a flawless projection, rather pasted together bits and pieces. It is as if the cosmos developed a design by which sensory inputs could be captured from the environment and continually stored in a holographic medium of virtually limitless storage capacity. Again, a deterministic system makes the process no less magical. There need not be a creator in any theological sense.

And if consciousness can be reduced in some respects to the parts that make up the inner theater, then consciousness may not be in itself so remarkable, but a commonplace potential, awaiting the right assemblage of parts in ripe circumstances to grow to notable proportions. In other words, it's possible consciousness, as we understand it, is a sharp focus of something that is ever-present. It's not a new idea, even in science. Respected physicist David Bohm believed all matter, even atoms, were conscious. He developed models describing reality unfolding from an unseen, or *implicate* order.[18]

One of the core traits of consciousness is its capacity for self-reflection. Someone can observe their own thoughts, then observe themselves observing them, ad infinitum, producing a potentially endless series of regressions in awareness. Massive collections of atoms in dynamic configurations can develop technology by which to analyze their more intricate parts. This is epitomized in a quote by quantum mechanics pioneer Neils Bohr, "A physicist is just an atom's way of looking at itself."[19]

If the brain can be reduced to an assemblage of parts that creates consciousness in the same way that a television produces an image, an-all-or nothing potential that requires everything to be in working order to operate at all, then the view that consciousness is fundamental to the universe is baseless. This is because it would only be produced by very precise configurations. But if the brain's design is a culminated from a continuous spectrum of *potential* for consciousness, a dim awareness that exists in every leaf, cell, rock, and atom, then the neurological reconstruction in our heads may be *the universe seeing its own thoughts*, and we do not end beyond what we can see.

Perhaps the universe tries to copy itself. Not in its entirety, but like our minds, in bits and pieces. We each recreate a small corner of the world. Even if it is far from a perfect copy, our personal stories occupy an illusionary inner expanse of fantastic proportions. Think of all the places you've ever been, a mental map charged with emotional associations.

The brain produces electrochemical signals that may at first seem random, but order emerges. We learn. Combined with the mobility a body provides, a wide range of information is taken in and processed into a copy of a tiny corner of the universe. In this light, the neurological reconstruction that manifests consciousness is a sort of reflector, made from the parts of the universe. The better the design, the more information and angles fed into it, the sharper the image. Our numbers and years as a species have given us the advantage of collectively coming to understand the world better by documenting what we learn, sharpening the image, making our situational awareness in the universe more comprehensive. If the internal reconstruction of the outside world is a sizeable part of who we are, and consciousness exists not as a rare and exceptional accident, but an ever-present sea of potential waiting to emerge, couldn't we just as easily say we are the universe pretending to be individuals? If our sense of identity and consciousness is attributed directly to this neurological reconstruction, couldn't it be argued that in some respect, we are also the universe looking in, the individualized sense of self seated behind windows to the outside world, merely a cheap parlor trick?

A newly born calf precariously raises itself on spindly legs, emitting a primal cry in spite of its small size. The universe put forth this cleverly orchestrated form, unfolded from a chemical template of dancing organizations with nearly perfect precision. The template itself is repetitious in nature, spawning consecutive copies while allowing for a small margin of error. The organic scaffolding is comprised of multiple systems locked together, each serving a different function, such as sustenance, mobility, and perception.

The universe is likewise born on this occasion, once more. The assemblage of parts suspended in ebb and flow was billions of years in the making, the elements themselves forged in the dying breaths of stars, billions of years more. Having eyes with which to see, this vehicle captures the visible light bouncing off the environment, converting it into situational awareness within a place setting. The universe is able to see.

Popular scientific thought maintains there is no intent behind the design that makes our existence possible, right down to the finely-tuned forces that keep the universe from flying apart. The tendency to anthropomorphize is understandable; after all, we view through human eyes. We try to comprehend everything in familiar terms borrowed from experience, projecting human attributes onto nature. The response against anthropic arguments is that we see patterns of deliberate design simply because it is in our nature.

A possible counterargument to anthropomorphizing involves how consciousness is defined in relation to things that are not conscious. The most hardline reductionist claims we are merely collections of parts, with only an illusion of free will. If consciousness and awareness are devalued, we are on equal footing with the universe as a whole, itself a collection of parts. Of course, that same reductionism would point to the cerebral cortex as the source of sentience, but it is really an insufficient explanation if consciousness is diffusely present throughout the universe, in even small amounts. The simple fact of the matter is that consciousness, though reasonably understood between one person and another, is only roughly defined and difficult to pin down conceptually.

And hypothetically, if we could have revealed to us the inner workings of the cosmos, how particles are connected without regard for following the rules of spacetime, would we feel comfortable redefining our hazy notions of consciousness to include it?

The bottom line is, if our consciousness is illusion we could feel free to project this onto the universe where we perceive elements of design. Even as an illusion, our consciousness is very real to us, and so it would be as a cosmic constant in our perception. Perhaps universal consciousness is somewhat a matter of individual perception. Maybe the safest premise in the middle of two extremes is that even just the appearance of anthropic principles is meaningful, at least keeping the door of possibility opened a crack. In a world of wacky quantum mechanics where reality at least *appears* to be reliant on observation, and where every perception is actually made of conscious thought in our heads, maybe the universe could be conscious because we are.

There is a dualistic nature to what most perceive as existence. The first component can be illustrated by a swirl of blocks, the components of matter, reaching up and tapering to a point of enormous complexity, the product of biological development over billions of years. The second component, we can imagine as a sort of ethereal whirlpool extending down to touch the first, resulting in an hourglass shape.

Whereas the swirl of blocks pointing upwards represents the physical universe we know of, the ethereal one pointing downward embodies a purposeful reality, the spiritual, unseen world that many claim to intuitively feel. This ethereal whirlpool could be depicted as organizing the physical construction of the universe. We see a correlation with this model and the hemispheres of the brain. As mentioned previously, the left half deals with particulars in analytical thinking, while the right puts information into context. A line of thought pertaining to metaphysical matters typically corresponds to the mind's expectation of a larger, unseen context surrounding one's own life.

If such a context exists, we can postulate that the material world of our everyday experience is an interior reality within a far vaster one. This larger reality would exceed the physical environment by leaps and bounds, but would also contain it. Religions and similar metaphysical belief systems apply symbols and ritual to the larger context to reinforce it as a reality in our lives, whether it is baptism in Christianity, prostration in Islam, or yoga in Hinduism. But like consciousness, it is difficult to pin down in this fashion.

It's important to keep in mind that ascribing consciousness as an immanent, fundamental attribute to the universe is merely hypothetical. Since the existence of a larger context rests on the point of consciousness being continuous, it is conjecture as well. Whatever appeal a metaphysical proposition involving consciousness might hold, we must remain vigilant, aware that this might promote favoritism and skew our perception.

But if a larger context exists at all, then surely it intervenes in our world by drawing gases together to form stars and forging heavy elements, which are then found recombining in persistent combinations to promote life.

In fairness to a framework accommodating science and spirituality, *both* must be acknowledged, no matter how absurd it seems. We are chemical processing factories in an evolutionary chain of events randomly thrown together over time, and consciousness is a product of our imaginings within a deterministic system.

We are also purposeful creatures sculpted by larger forces within a timeless eternity adjacent to the physical world, which is, in itself, a knitted patchwork quilt of conscious activity. This *equal grounds premise* between science and spirituality ensures that on the whole, one is never considered more valid than the other. Of course, it depends on the subject matter to which they are being applied. In studying the efficiency of windmill designs, or treating disease, science is the clear and proven choice of method. In contrast, struggling to overcome addiction, finding a new direction in life, or mourning a lost loved one would all fall under the purview of things spiritual. And while the methods of science are not in question, it is only the ever-present *possibility* of a generalized spiritual framework that cannot be dismissed. This could be perceived as an unbalanced relationship between two concepts alleged to have equal legitimacy. The spiritual context proposed in this exploratory alliance constitutes either future science that has not yet been discovered, or an actuality which science is not equipped to find on its own. The sheer scale of what could lie beyond in this larger context, a more expansive, unending presence outside the confines of spacetime, arguably makes it a contender to the fundamentals of science, even in conjecture. The notion of a larger reality presented throughout this book is a barebones spirituality stripped of nonessentials, and based on a single repeating principle, that being consciousness.

The calf enjoys its days beneath the sun, grows old, and dies. We know what happens to its body, but what of its mind, its identity? Does it continue to consciously perceive? If we are in actuality this larger reality taking form within this material realm, a simulation, perhaps, then would all our experiences and sense of self merely vanish away? Or is it not a matter of losing ourselves to nonexistence, but realizing our larger selves on the way back to our source?

We cannot help but see ourselves in human terms: driving to work, eating dinner, walking the dog, or engaged in conversation. A conscious agency of entirely different constitution and background looking down upon our comparatively meager civilization might view streaming lines of ground and air traffic in the same light that we would see ants carrying resources back to their anthill. Each individual has a destination in mind and motivations for going there.

By the same token, that independent entity would likely not make the same connections we do catching a glimpse of a smile, or a snippet of conversation. These might be as imperceptible to our observer as chemical signals in nature are to us.

When we look at another's eyes, for example, these "windows to the soul" are considered the ultimate expression of who a person is. An outsider unfamiliar with the development of life on earth would probably not readily know an eye from a toe.

The perspective of humanity, or complex life, is in a way hampered by our view from inside it. Instead of speaking of human beings, let us disentangle ourselves from the familiar assumptions and narrow, daily experience of our species.

In a hypothetical world, an unusual species of plant holds a core of spectacular complexity. This mass is comprised of microscopic threads of different lengths that transmit electrochemical signals. These threads also branch off into smaller threads, the overall connections numbering in the quadrillions. Yet this core mass is not much larger than an outstretched hand. With special equipment accompanying the thought experiment, we see what is going on inside these plants. Signals mix at an amazing speed, while partitions and bridges appear and fall away as patterns emerge. Blossoms within blossoms unfold from this electromagnetic symphony faster than the eye can follow. Vibrations of sound and light from the environment outside the plants seem to feed the repository of stored signals, though the kaleidoscope patterns continue to emerge even in sensory darkness. Dotting the landscape worldwide, these mysterious plants communicate and mentally plan. And there are subtle indications that the plants are aware they are doing all of this. Make them instead animal-kind with mobility and prehensile skills to manipulate their environment, and it could be us we are describing.

What would the universe want of these creatures? How is it that this organ within them, this "brain," can consistently produce patterns of unimaginable complexity? One can argue that an apple is partly made of carbohydrates, which are themselves made of atoms, but the emptiness inside those individual atoms has no bearing on the solidity of the apple in the macroworld. The outermost electron shells of these atoms repelling against one another create what we experience as solidity. The subatomic realms of these atoms certainly don't reflect the genetic blueprint of the apple. They likewise have no bearing on the flavor or texture of the apple. As we zoom out, the information picture changes. A similar argument can be made on the matter of consciousness. The conventional line of reasoning tells us many of the atoms that constitute us form the molecular machinery of cellular processes. In the circuitry of the brain these cells form entire regions, working together in an orchestrated manner to create the phenomenon we call consciousness. But what if the latter part of this reasoning is flawed, and consciousness is more than an emergent property from a particular assemblage of parts?

If Bohm and those supporting his views were correct, then even with the tiniest possible amount of consciousness attributed to an atom, the universe would be brimming with it. A part of our difficulty in understanding this concept is that we relate our daily activities with a certain level of self-awareness. Probably the closest approximation with lesser consciousness we can easily relate to is the twilight between waking and sleep states. Cut this awareness in half several thousand times and you still have something rather than nothing, it could be argued, a matter of degrees as opposed to the definitive "true or false" determination.

An atom or molecule by itself would present a negligible amount of consciousness in this line of thinking, but there's a lot of matter in just the known universe. If there is any consciousness at all in this grand scenario, a conservative estimate might put it in familiar terms as collectively only faintly aware.

But let's keep in mind that science views all frames of time to be valid, and it is only our perspective that changes as we appear to move within it. We walk with dinosaurs; they are merely in a different time frame. It's reasonable to surmise that a universal collective consciousness wouldn't be bound by spacetime, as we seem to be. With countless information feeds pouring in from all existence, indeed, all realities that could take place, it's feasible this animating principle could surpass the dimly aware state, easily dwarfing ours in comparison. Perhaps universal consciousness could be described as a great expanse of ocean. With only the dimmest awareness at the surface, the density of consciousness increases as we move deeper into this *information universe*. The molecular machinery we call life and the development of sophisticated neurology create an event horizon, allowing this deeper consciousness to emerge into our reality.

And if consciousness is not a natural characteristic of matter, then humans, animals, and insects, all manners of flying, fleeting, burrowing fauna and perhaps flora, are lanterns exploring the deep well of unknown. They are conscious within a universe that would explore itself, one that it is otherwise blind to. We are part of the universe, not separate. We are complex configurations of the same stuff found anywhere else. We are pools of order riding self-replicating templates in a sea of entropy.

As the equal ground premise would have it, perhaps the question is not so simple as one or the other. Like some metaphysical circus performer, we are forced to juggle two concepts simultaneously as we stare up at the starry sky, contemplating if there is a sense of meaning to life. To clarify, it is not so much a case of not knowing which of the two perspectives is correct, but accepting them both. It flies in the face of reason to hold two contradictory premises. It would seem that either one or the other is correct, not both at the same time. Perhaps there is a way of building a bridge between the two, placing reductionism and universal consciousness into a context where both can reside.

Imagine an individual has a dream they are in a car accident, and later that day, it happens. The spiritualist might call the dream a premonition of the event, while the skeptic would likely proclaim the event a self-fulfilling prophecy set into motion by the dream. In the event neither is exclusively correct, this might mean a context outside spacetime is interacting with the physical world in a process we might call *attunement.* Like the swirl of blocks tapering to meet a conscious whirlwind, the point where they intersect is everything we can consciously perceive as real in the present moment. This attunement is how a brain's activity can be locked within a deterministic system, *and* be shaped by a corresponding larger consciousness. Evidence can point to physical origins and development of the universe, and cosmologists have accumulated a great deal of corroborating data confirming the present model. Thirteenth-century theologian Thomas Aquinas similarly believed the universe must have been produced from an "uncaused first cause" (which he attributed to God). But, contrary to our commonsense notions, a beginning may exist to some extent in appearance only.

To separate the material universe from the larger reality, this physical reality must be given the appearance of self-sufficiency from inside the system. In other words, in order to manipulate the material world from the larger context, those actions must be described in the language of the material world.

Of course, because of the nature of the equal ground premise, this dichotomy is only a potential. A larger conceptual framework surrounds it, in which the knowledge science has gained about a predictable, natural world is not disputed. The spiritualist viewpoint cannot be objectively verified, but it can also never be dismissed. Again, merely an acknowledgment of the potential for this larger context to exist is all that is needed, and the degree of its acceptance is a personal choice.

Signals of varying frequencies from the outside world bombard our senses. From these signals, we construct an interior representation of the environment.

One could construe this process as a constant communication to them from the outside world. Conventional thinking has it that other minds communicate with us through means such as speech and writing, and the process stops there. But on some rudimentary level of the mind, all incoming input could be construed as some form of communication, the universe speaking to that individual. Higher brain functions and situational awareness sort through these patterns, determining what could pertain to them personally, and what is just random noise or subconscious chatter. But some could feel that all of their experience is the outside world communicating directly with them, entire events set as lessons with knowledge to be gained from them.

We are intelligent beings, having come a long way recently in understanding how our minds can trick us. For perception of the outside world to be construed as communication with us, it would require that the source was also intelligent. Such awareness would likely extend far beyond our own, perhaps even being ascribed as omniscient (all-knowing), while the ability to shape the events that happen to us might be described as omnipotent (all-powerful). Trust that this communication came from a reliable source would demonstrate belief in an additional quality: omnibenevolence, or having only our best interests at heart. There is also the issue of the communication itself. For instance, today's newer computers have difficulty communicating with much earlier generations of computers, which may seem counterintuitive. One might expect the more comprehensive system to be more capable in every way, without the comparative slowness of the other system reflecting on the interaction. In the same respect, a higher power might be limited in presenting a message by *our own* limitations. The available information set, that being symbols and events we would be able to recognize and process, would have to suffice. To illustrate, a single-celled organism in a petri dish could be nudged in one direction or another, but the information we were able to share with it would be extremely limited. This may shed light on why some often make the same mistakes in life repeatedly before finally reaching a place of contentment. In this case, the hands of divine providence are effectively tied by the finite abilities of our design.

But it's important to keep in mind the likely timeless state of such intelligence, and how a lifetime would appear to unfold from that perspective in the wink of an eye. Perhaps the sometimes arduous passage of time is our perception, a reflection of our finite capacities, and not the communication process as a whole.

In extrapolating how the generalized spiritual framework unfolds, it might become more apparent how this communication could work. A theistic or deistic interpretation of a higher power may be difficult to represent, as the inherent symbolism that distinguishes one religion from another would conflict with the freeform expectations of the framework as a whole. Were this higher power represented as a consciousness comprising the entirety of existence (pantheism), it would be difficult to pin down mentally without using symbols, although forms of meditation where the mind is cleared may facilitate this. The closest representation of a higher power, with respect to the spiritual framework of the equal ground premise, may be the larger self, or soul. Since a higher power is typically viewed through the lens of one's personality, the god concept subject to qualia, some spiritualists may inadvertently practice this subtle communication with a larger aspect of themselves under a guise of speaking with the divine.

FIVE

Prometheus Unbound

The Landscape of a Larger Reality

Perhaps above all else, everyone has a secret longing that others could see their soul, in all its splendor.

At the 2011 World Science Festival, a panel of prominent physicists and computer scientists discussed the idea of the universe being something like a computer.[20] One postulate was that the space between two people having a conversation was largely irrelevant, and that the information being exchanged was the fundamental reality. This is an interesting idea to be explored on our own, purely hypothetically, of course.

Imagine two people are having a conversation, face-to-face, over the phone, or online. In this respect, we could say the sharing window, or *link,* between those people, is open. This would suggest we couldn't communicate to a particular street vendor in Argentina on a whim, because the link is closed. The same could be said of someone who cannot be reached because their phone battery has gone dead, or a neighbor who is not answering their door. Distance is irrelevant in these scenarios. All that matters is that there is a means whereby the information can be passed along. But how can information be more real than physical objects?

It is like taking a simple, online chat room and expanding on it. Instead of letters on computer screens, we could have a virtual environment with bodies, people seated in chairs, just for the purpose of elaborating on the way the information, in this case the conversation, is conveyed back and forth. There is greater freedom of expression. The characters within this environment can use facial expressions, voice modulations, body language, or simply rise up out of their chairs and dramatically walk out, just to better express themselves. The extra information adds to the conversation.

Physicist Tom Campbell proposes life in our universe is something like a computer simulation. He proposes the analogy of a video game, wherein the avatar exists within a virtual environment. This computer-generated landscape only exists in the direction the character is looking (bearing similarity to what quantum mechanics suggests about the real world), while the person playing the character is not actually inside the game at all.[21]

How would one describe an apple? Is it red, or perhaps green? Is it roughly rounded in shape? Is it a fruit? The answer is yes, yes, and yes. It is actually many things by way of association, yet the descriptions do not contradict each other. When we see an apple, our minds instantly reference the image with everything we know about apples, not just aspects of their physical appearance, but taste, smell, texture, how to bake them in a pie, even related characters like George Washington and Sir Isaac Newton. This is the power of association, knitting information into patterns. And like snowflakes, no pattern is ever quite the same against the ever-dynamic background of the subconscious.

Like the cat walking across a chessboard, an infant does not see a chair quite like we do. Lines, curves, and patterns merge into an associative blur, maybe even a bit of a blind spot. Unlike the cat, the child comes to know the nature of the chair over time, by standing on it, by sitting, realizing how its four legs keep it from toppling over, understanding it in both form and function. Theoretically, when an adult sees the chair, it instantly associates the image with all the chairs we've encountered in our lifetime, a quick cross-reference in the subconscious under an associative category we might simply call *chair.* Though we are not aware of the process, it does happen.

Many ideas of how the cosmos came into being start out with creation by a supreme being, or *ex nihilo,* out of nothing. The cosmic egg is a mythological icon found in creation myths in many cultures. The Big Bang theory describes how the universe exploded from a miniscule, but dense, clump of material. The more modern component of this, known as the inflationary model, has the universe beginning with a tiny quantum fluctuation, practically nothing at all.

Imagine that at the beginning, there was a primordial pattern, a *root nest* of information. For illustration, one could construe it as something analogous to thought, like the example of the apple. This tightly woven pattern began to differentiate within itself, trains of associative links mowing through the previously unbroken wholeness of the root nest, expanding upon its theme, previously penned-up potentials unbounded. Like a Big Bang, but of information, though nothing ever actually moves. Forms coalesce, apparent divisions set up, forming differing regions. It's quite possible that through a sort of runaway, trickle-down effect, this process would produce the physical universe we are familiar with, and likely many other information pattern environments operating under different sets of rules. Space and time could be manifestations of our particular set of rules, the explosion of information being simultaneous, or outside our familiar spacetime construct. This would mean this hypothetical version of the Big Bang happens at every point of space, throughout all of time.

"Where did the initial body of information come from?" one might ask. Recall that this hypothetical process is simultaneous, nested within our own existence. Existing itself outside of time, there would be no beginning.

"Is it purposeful?" we might ask. "Is there a focused intent behind it?" This opens the door for an interesting comparison. An independent observer might see all the strife in the world, based in territoriality, conflicting beliefs, and fear. They might then look randomly through our shared depository of knowledge, the internet. It is unquestionably a valuable resource, a forum for the sharing of ideas, many links available, and yet, it might seem a bit unfocused, even scattered. The observer might then ask, "Are we purposeful?" We are conscious beings, after all. Is there a guideline to measure this? It is entirely possible that any creative process behind the universe is as scatterbrained as we are. Or, from our view from inside time, the universe could always have the appearance of being a work *under construction.* This model of the beginning requires, at the very least, a rudimentary consciousness to discriminate between one thing and another, enough for the associative start-up routine to begin. Science understandably steers clear of this approach based in consciousness, especially if something resembling an emotional component to the process is suggested.

The problem with criticism of this model is our own intellectual shortcomings. Because this hypothetical process of creation lay outside of time, it is also removed from the cause and effect relationships we use to identify with logical processes in the world. We see again the familiar theme of the psychological realm giving birth to matter, an initial parcel of *cosmic thought*, appearing as if in a causal loop, creating itself. But we must remind ourselves that this description is of a possible reality outside of time. It *would* be unfamiliar. Not to the workings of the mind so much as what we expect from the material world. Perhaps what could be construed by skeptical minds as clichéd and predictable might also account for the existence of anything at all, which is anything but clichéd. The perceived need for a first cause of the universe may be the limits of our neurology. We can describe time using terminology based in that mutual understanding, but we don't actually know what time is. There could be multiple dimensions of time. The passage of time could be an associative thread through the multiverse that we only are only neurologically hardwired to perceive as linear. Physicist John Wheeler proposed quantum phenomena could actually create the past from the present,[22] and experiments since have shown some particles can reach backwards through time. If we can establish reasonable doubt because the brain is metaphorically trapped in a fishbowl, with no conceptual vision outside its capabilities involving time, no argument involving the need for causality behind the universe can be airtight.

Referring back to the gaming analogy, there is a disparity between relative timelines. The game can be started a number of times. Beginning from a preprogrammed point, a character within the game would be none the wiser. Having no memory with which to keep count, each time would seem like the first. From the perspective of the individual playing the game on the outside, the character within inhabits a *floating timeline*, wherein each time the game begins, the computer-generated character has no idea *when* it is *outside* the game. Even if the character had an awareness of what was going on, the environment outside the game would still appear as simultaneous potentials. From the character's deterministic frame of reference, the notion of outside time might appear as a pinwheel of indefinite time periods intersecting with its own, seemingly one-time game activation.

The idea of the physical universe extending into an endless information universe is highly speculative, for a number of reasons. Firstly, it is a subject on something that can't be measured, bringing us to our second point: the nature of information itself. In information theory, there is an abstract component, but also a physical component. A book can convey ideas through the symbols on its pages. Even though the reader must be a conscious being and understand the language in order to interpret the story, the book itself (or some physical delivery system) is a necessity in this process. The notion that the physical universe is tucked into a tiny corner of a spiritual universe is a common theme in Eastern religions and New Age thought. While an information model corresponding to a universe full of matter is generally acceptable to science, a more expansive spiritual universe connected to each person is not. Still, if it is an endless web of association, then ultimately, nothing is separate. Every object might be a distant link to any other.

The third difficulty with the endless information universe lies not with its veracity as much as our ability to describe it. Take a smartphone for example. It can access information through extensive networks, take pictures, play music, even message or speak to people over vast distances. The phone itself is miniaturized integrated circuitry with layers upon layers of complex programming. The wafers in these billions of nanosized transistors have become so thin that developers constantly seek new materials in this miniaturization process to keep the electron from jumping through to the other side, a phenomenon known as quantum tunneling.[23] We cannot see the intricate signals going to and from the phone, nor could we come close to building one even with the raw resources at hand. A multitude of industries take part in the material acquisition and refinement, assembly, and programming.

If you took a smartphone or similar high-tech device back to the 1980s, people of that generation would be bowled over. Even without cell towers or internet, the incredible clarity of its liquid crystal display, touchscreen technology, and unimaginable storage capacity for pictures, music, and games would put primitive recording mediums and gaming systems to shame. Large corporations in the electronics industry would likely consider the item priceless. Although immediate replication wouldn't be possible due to the lack of manufacturing techniques, just what they could learn from taking it apart and examining the parts would take them in entirely new directions.

In the 1960s, just having transitioned from vacuum tubes to solid-state technology, they'd call it science fiction. The processing power of the Apollo 11 lunar module's onboard computer was comparable to that of a calculator.

Many centuries ago, denizens of preindustrial Earth would call it magic, or witchcraft, while thousands of years ago they might think you a god if you produced a smartphone.

The point is that as our technology increases, the analogies we apply to the universe get better. The more we understand, the better we are able to formulate approximations of a larger truth to our existence. But it's possible that outside the simple representations available to us, the answers we seek are simply beyond our comprehension for the present. In such a case, a computer program analogy could be the correct course, but still likely do little to convey how advanced an information universe based in consciousness would really be.

The universe has been developing for billions of years. It has long-practiced resources to create complex building materials, and assembly of those chemical elements into life is a process we are still trying to grasp. Albeit our intellectual capacities make comparatively quick work of piecing together the cosmic puzzle, it has a huge head start on us. The assertion that the physical world works by information and probability gives depth to a computer program analogy, though again, our familiar example probably pales in comparison to the actual case. If the analogy is at least pointed in the right direction, then an intelligence underlying the universe could be as far beyond us as the capabilities of a smartphone are beyond those of an abacus. The formation of stars, processing the very lightest of atomic elements into heavier ones, could appear as a sort of *update* to this cosmic program. The subsequent formation of life, then intelligence, could also be viewed as updates. Of course, this presupposes these changes did not lay nested into the early universe as it unfolded, like the genetic material hidden away within a flower. Again, we see what appear to be the opposing views of inherent design and outside intervention, echoing those of random accident versus purposeful intent.

Thought processes such as these form the basis of belief systems, mixtures of one hemispheric viewpoint or the other, with symbols applied to these mental constructs in a series of tiers representing conclusions. Some create a set of beliefs and claim it embodies all possible knowledge, even while a multitude of alternate configurations are possible. Some of these constructs are wobbly or lopsided, threatening to fall in a cloud of fallacies and assumptions, while practicing members gather around and hold it up. This is because as incredibly stable as the tiers of science are, consisting more of facts based on repeated observation and testing than personal beliefs, it cannot alone frame the big picture. It cannot give people meaning. Some are simply forced to use whatever belief system is available, picking from a worldly assortment at best, or, at worst, settling with what their culture provides as the only option.

Once again, we must follow a call to reason and return from the realm of hypotheticals, compelling as they may be. Where there is ambiguity, the equal grounds premise would have us at least acknowledge both the view of a universal consciousness, and that in which there is none.

Beyond the limit of those things we know for sure, we must reserve judgment. With our head in the clouds, we must remain anchored to Earth. If we delve into the spirit of science fiction, however, giving ourselves license to imagine the enormous consequences of such a universe, that brilliant object in the sky that propelled life on Earth could be a good place to start. The ancient Egyptians and Sumerians worshipped the Sun as a god. The Greek philosopher Anaxagoras proposed it was a scorching hot stone. Modern science knows the Sun to be an average star, a massive ball of superheated plasma undergoing fusion. Recall that the particles that make up our world exhibit properties that ignore the constraints of spacetime whenever it's convenient, possibly indicating a larger field of activity. If there is a complex coordination to this unseen reality underlying our own, perhaps a sort of *cosmic software*, what does this mean for the Sun? Our home star is by far the largest object anywhere near the Earth. It is the center of activity for light years around, and it is absolutely massive beyond description. If the case of corresponding software beneath the physical stage were true, the Sun would undoubtedly be more than just a ball of superheated plasma. In such a circumstance, the

Sun could be viewed as a local server in this deep ocean of cosmic software. Its physical presence would be likened to the display on a calculator, while the real activity takes place beyond the universe as we understand it. The Sun that lights our skies would be far beyond reach, but everything within its sphere of influence would lie within its software.

And what might it be like from a privileged vantage point in this proposed information universe based in consciousness? Some spiritualists would consider a larger personality inevitable in a consciousness-based universe. Regardless, the following can be thought of as pure fiction resting on a hypothetical. It is merely an attempt to capture a glimpse of what existing in such a larger reality might be like.

Imagine gazing down from a mountaintop at all of existence, you have a larger mind, but not necessarily some nirvana-like immersion in everything. Existing in a more spacious environment, the larger mind is like the adult who was once the child. It is something that belongs to you, personal and familiar, experienced and wiser. It's quite possible you are one of many personalities created within this larger one. In such a scenario, each life is an information packet, unzipped as it is experienced with a set of challenges in the world; you exist side by side with them. It would know you well, for it could be said that this larger self is what you would become. The larger personality's wishes for the individual would likely be character development and acquisition of knowledge. In this spacious environment, you could see so much more of cosmos, its body and depths. It would be like having your own Hubble Space Telescope, your own Cambridge Library.

You would be like a child playing with blocks of worldly consequence. You may create your own simulations and pocket universes, playing with physical laws and different manners of neurological perception. There exist a practical infinity of apps in endless subjects to assist in this creation process. Like a cosmic tide, waves of joy and pleasure crash over you again and again, and you realize with elation that this freedom of creative play is your natural state. And there is beauty, such beauty.

It's a big *if.* But were it true, such an existence would culminate the best of all possible worlds. A more comprehensive, even wiser identity with enormous freedoms fits the model of a generalized spiritual framework. With respect to the equal grounds premise, it presents as an all-or-nothing proposition where complex ideologies don't easily apply.

SIX

Chrysalis
Testimonials of Distant Lands

The body is the mask we wear. The true depth of our character cannot fit within these cramped and narrow spaces any more than the sky can display all the stars.

On the morning of February 2, 2006, Anita Moorjani was rushed to the hospital, having fallen into a coma. Diagnosed with cancer of the lymphatic system a few years before, she had refused chemotherapy and became riddled with large tumors inside her body. As she lay dying in a coma with total organ failure, she reportedly witnessed the attempts to save her life from outside her body. This one vantage point expanded to envelop people and places around her, as if she had become those things. She saw her brother on a plane coming to see her and overheard conversations elsewhere in the hospital. The experience that follows she describes in her book, *Dying to be Me*, as ". . . a huge, dark warehouse . . . with only one flashlight to see by. Everything you know about what's contained within this enormous space is what you've seen by the beam of one small flashlight."[24] This captivating account provides a sense of much larger scales than we are normally accustomed to. She goes on to say:

> That is what physical life is like. We're only aware of what we focus our senses on at any given time, and we can only understand what is already familiar. Next, imagine that one day, someone flicks on a switch. There for the first time, in a sudden burst of brilliance and sound and color, you can see the entire warehouse, and it's nothing like anything you'd ever imagined.
> The vastness, complexity, depth, and breadth of everything going on around you is almost overwhelming. You can't see all the way to the end of space, and you know there's more to it than what you can take in from this torrent that's tantalizing your senses and emotions. But you do get a strong feeling that you're actually part of something alive, infinite, and altogether fantastic, that you are part of a large and unfolding tapestry that goes beyond sight and sound.[25]

Moorjani's claims about her experience are sensational, but not uncommon. All the documented cases of the Near-Death Experience, or *NDE,* constitute only a smidgen of all the tales involving brushes with mortality since humans began walking the Earth.

In the book *The Holographic Universe*, physicist Michael Talbot painted an engaging picture of a boundless universe permeated by consciousness. He presented documented cases of paranormal events, while focusing on ideas like Bohm's Implicate Order to provide a framework that could accommodate them. While presenting cases of NDEs, he cited a 1981 Gallop poll in which eight million Americans claimed to have had their own NDE. That's nearly one out of every twenty adults. He goes on to explain that these experiences cross cultural boundaries, and recorded accounts date back well into early human history.[26]

On the subject of NDEs, many medical professionals (though by no means all) allege there is a very small degree of electrical activity deep inside the brain, even in what appears to be brain death, beyond the detection range of EEGs, and that this is the source of the experiences claimed. They further assert that the mind frantically concocts stories in its last moments to give it a sense of well-being.

It's unreasonable to disagree with experts in their field. By using the products of science, we are, in a sense, obligated to trust those educated in it to formulate the best answers according to the available knowledge. A layman disputing the position of the medical community might be a bit like a passenger arguing with the pilot on how to fly the plane. But when those experts disagree amongst themselves, especially on epistemological matters with regards to the nature of consciousness, we are free to choose sides while using our best judgment. Please note it is not my intention to attempt to provide evidence of life after death; there are serious researchers better equipped for such tasks. My aim is merely to present a consistency between NDEs and the conceptual model of the generalized spiritual framework, in the hopes that the organizational relationships of ideas appear coherent overall.

NDEs are frequently reported as vivid, even more so than daily experiences. NDEers often describe themselves as fully conscious, with situational awareness of themselves within an environment. But even dreaming requires a notable and measurable amount of brain activity, as do hallucinations.[27] And NDEs are described as powerful, life-changing experiences. This seems inconsistent with the explanation of undetectable brain activity beyond the reach of EEGs. In many documented accounts, NDEers report information not readily available to them. They may describe procedures performed or conversations so far outside their immediate environment, and sometimes of such detail, that the explanation of mental creativity isn't applicable.[28]

A trademark of most experiences is an overwhelming feeling of unconditional love, while a small fraction of experiences can be unpleasant.[29] Despite individual variations in the experiences, there are common themes, such as experiencing a feeling of tranquility, moving through a tunnel, encountering a being of light, and the life review, wherein the individual views the entirety of their life down to the tiniest details.[30] Science maintains that perfectly good explanations exist for these phenomena. The tunnel and bright light, for example, are reportedly the optical effects produced by an oxygen-deprived retina.[31] But recall the concept of attunement, wherein information must be translated into the cause and effect language of the physical world. If it is seen, there must be a visual component. In this light, the initial experiences viewed as being divorced from reductionism aren't necessarily dependent on the physical system at all, but use it, perhaps to convey meaning.

The reductionist's anticipated reaction to this explanation would surely be that it is the ultimate avoidance. For a rational explanation to be given, and simultaneously dismissed as unrelated because "another system is in play" certainly seems evasive. If we relate this example to the character in a video game, however, we can mentally picture that when we decide to storm the castle (or whatever goals the game provides), the only way to achieve this is by using the character in the game. We cannot physically reach into the screen and storm the castle ourselves. The game field is an encapsulated reality, a visual expression of programming. The only way to access that programming is via the keyboard, mouse, or game controller we are using as an interface with that program. In similar fashion, the reported NDE is within the bounds of the game's programming until such time as the player leaves the game, and the electrical activity of the character fizzles out. Once the brain no longer possesses sufficient electrical activity to explain the expansive nature of the experience, it can then be argued another system is in play. Then the intent behind creating and motivating the character has reintegrated to the outside world, or, in this case, the larger reality, which is no longer interfacing with the interior reality. The easy way to avoid magical thinking is to trust there is usually a rational explanation to unexplained phenomena, but this doesn't discount a correspondence with some kind of spiritual system.

This brings us to another question, concerning the idea of a one-to-one correspondence between the content of the experience, and the frame of mind perceiving it. To clarify, an image from a slide projected onto a screen is a one-to-one correspondence. At every point, the information maintains the same organizational relationships. The image from the outside world reconstructed in the brain does not have a one-to-one correspondence, because this information is reassembled through differentiated neural processes. Some features are highlighted, while others are discarded as irrelevant.

In the case of NDEs, the one-to-one correspondence refers to the frame of reference. Can the brain create the sense of a larger space than we normally experience? And most pertinently, could an oxygen-deprived, failing brain convince itself that its experience fit the definition of a vast environment? Or, could the brain fill in these perceptions after the fact while remembering? Again falling under the purview of epistemological philosophy, this is a difficult question to answer. Asking if the picture is actually complex, or is that quality merely *inferred*, is a bit like asking if water is *really* wet, or if this is just our perception of it. But it is a possibility we must keep in mind if we want to maintain an honest worldview with respect to skepticism.

Overall, it's not likely one can make a definitive assessment that all parties could accept. The reductionist would undoubtedly stick to the model in which conscious is a phenomenon generated solely by the brain, while the spiritualist follows an intuition that there is a larger environment or being that is connected to them personally. Both could use the consistencies between NDEs to validate their position. What is called for is a hint of reasonable doubt *on both sides.* It conjures up the image of a hung jury where eleven jurors vote for their preferred verdict, while one holds out due to insufficient evidence. For the reductionist, this single juror could represent the possibility of a larger context for an individual's consciousness in the form of a runaway information universe. For the spiritualist, the dissenting vote could be the acknowledgement that thoroughly accepted dogma about the universe had been shown to be inconsistent with scientific discovery countless times.

The generalized spiritual framework predicts a larger personality, embodying all the individual is, and more. This implies not simply a linear progression beyond death, but a continuation beyond life in *scale*. In other words, that larger aspect of that person would exist simultaneously before birth and after death. Life is like a story written by the larger self, in which the author exists outside the story. In this sense, the larger personality is as much a projection of the individual as well as vice-versa.

In the funnel illustration, the moment of conscious perception would expand upon death to encompass the life completely. This is consistent with the life review, where an individual sees their life in its entirety. This moment also inflates past the life boundary into the surrounding larger context, the realm of the larger personality. Whereas some may feel as if awakening from a dream, others may hold onto familiar constructs of everyday life, making the transition more challenging. It stands to reason this larger self could appear as a comforting figure, perhaps taking the shape of a religious entity, or deceased relative. Such benevolent deception could also be fabricated by the larger reality itself. There might be a concerted effort in finding ways to acclimate the returning consciousness to the far vaster environment.

A key feature these NDEs share is the individual often encounters circumstances that were anticipated. For example, in a hypothetical car crash on the way to church, one parishioner may encounter a lake of fire and brimstone, while another meets Jesus. Both survive, later relating their tales to each other and the members of their church the following

Sunday. All these people would take the stories as adding credibility to their expectations of the afterlife and their religion in general.

However, when people of other cultures and belief systems encounter different religious figures and circumstances, say, a Hindu who encounters Lord Rama in a setting resembling one from Vedic mythology, we encounter the mutual exclusivity issue that comes with viewing different religions side by side. One could postulate that each experience is subjectively real in each individual case, which would ordinarily relegate it the inner world of mental experiences. But introducing a larger reality component to consciousness, this imagining could be displayed onto a great stage of practically limitless capacity.

Upon death, the exterior environment having been removed, the conscious mind looks into the subconscious as its new environment: this is the model presented by the generalized spiritual framework, insomuch as the deeper mind is viewed as the conduit to the larger personality. As in a state of deep hypnosis, or lucid dreaming, the mind can return to a place of freeform creativity. In what we can think of as a *default state* of the mind, every thought instantly materializes into exterior experience. The determining factors in how this unfolds are the filters we have in place psychologically, namely our beliefs and expectations. It stands to reason that if one genuinely expects a religious figure, family member, or even a place of punishment, his or her mind will create this as they pass the life boundary of the funnel. Such imaginings are likely temporary as they are tools for acclimating the individual personality back to the larger realm. Some may not require a guided reintroduction to that larger environment, but instead, intimately recall how it works. Such a consciousness could create freely, becoming or experiencing anything they desire. With respect to the view of consciousness inherent in the generalized spiritual framework, the outward projection of imagination into reality could stand as the rule of our existence, not the exception.

It's important to note that even if these NDE claims were not actually examples of consciousness existing independent of the brain, this does not rule out life beyond death. The generalized spiritual framework suggests that we occupy two very different environments with regard to time: the linear time we experience in life, and the simultaneity of time in the larger context. At life's conclusion, we would appear to simply return to that larger identity, but from its perspective, we are already in its midst. That we are not directly aware of this larger environment does not indicate it does not exist, or that it will always be beyond our reach. It's also worth noting that other potentials of self are possible beyond the larger one. Implementing the holographic principle, wherein each part carries a blueprint of the whole, the entirety of existence could lie within all of us.

There are many instances from around the world where children tell of their former lives in precise, often verifiable detail, constituting for some body of evidence. In his book *Children Who Remember Past Lives,* professor of psychology Ian Stevenson details his research of past life claims.[32] He clarifies that a belief in reincarnation is not limited to Eastern religions such as Hinduism or Buddhism, but exists to some degree in many belief systems throughout the world.[33] Also, he points out that those purporting reincarnation did not always indicate the concept of *karma* as a struggle for spiritual advancement.[34]

A quick search online reveals a plethora of contradictory metaphysical and spiritual particulars on reincarnation, numbered levels of advancement and so forth that we can write off due to mutual exclusivity.

The generalized spiritual framework does not directly imply the existence of reincarnation, as it isn't an expression of a larger self in a more expansive reality. This requires a second step, visualizing the playing field of life from that higher vantage point. Simplifying the funnel of consciousness, this relationship could be illustrated by an inverted pyramid. The point on which it rests is the individual self in time, who conceptually looks up to a greater representation of themselves in a corresponding larger environment. Turning the pyramidal illustration, the larger personality at the apex, overtop a broad base, does seem to suggest the larger personality could create a great number of individual expressions from outside time.

The idea of incarnating as other people may seem a bit silly, unless you look at life as being a learning experience. Then it makes a certain amount of sense. After a time, we become settled into a set of beliefs about the world, about people, and become slow to change. By creating and playing out characters a handful of times, with different abilities in circumstances wrought with distinctive challenges, one would gain a unique and well-rounded view on the human experience, all the while meeting familiar soul friends again and again in various types of relationships. It's a beautiful idea. One could make the analogy that in a larger reality we go to school, attending classes in various subjects. Some of these courses are more basic to the human experience, required credits, while some lesson plans or studies are more specialized.

Under this premise, we are all here doing our own thing. In this, there is a place beyond good and evil, beyond judgment, where even mortal enemies serve to play a role in teaching life lessons.

Reincarnation would not simply be a matter of jumping from one body to the next, if that were even possible. In a New Age interpretation popularized by author Jane Roberts, incarnations exist simultaneously outside of time, while the individual personality perceives themselves as moving from one life to the next, in continuity.[35] This concurs with the principle of attunement presented earlier in this book, in which a consciousness perceiving time interacts with a timeless state. The fact that NDEers often encounter guides before being sent back to Earth would seem to indicate we go first to our source, regardless of what follows. From within that larger mind, in whatever guise it takes for our benefit, we select from candidates, seeking out particular circumstances and potentials of an unfolding life that meet with our requirements. Sometimes family members, friends, and associates are known from other performances scattered through time. As if sitting before a keyboard, we access the relevant information. We perform searches and plan to meet old acquaintances. It takes place outside this reality, an environment that seems intimately familiar, quickly becoming second nature.

We are attached to our lives and the people we love. We define ourselves largely by our experiences in the world. But imagine for a moment the idea of *being someone else.* Having lived a full life, with a relatively clear conscience and sense of accomplishment rooted in personal growth, envision starting out with a clean slate. Picture being able to design a *vacation life* devoted to pure enjoyment, after a particularly rough one, or series of challenging lives. You create a template with free-flowing expectations for happiness. As you focus more on the details, your consciousness integrates more strongly into each of the moments at the bottom of the funnel. In the same fashion that the brain pastes together a picture of reality, you knit together a series of events into continuity. Plummeting into the emotional depths, you begin to believe you are really there. But you are also outside of that life, peering in, moving events around and planning to meet people, some of whom you already know. You are the author. Previous (and future) incarnations would be nothing more than distant, unconscious memories, even as they exist side by side with you in a multidimensional gallery of the larger self, in which each personality continues to blossom. Were all of this simply frivolous imaginings, it's still a lovely idea.

One of the world's best feelings is meeting a dear friend whom you haven't seen for a couple hundred years.

SEVEN

The Wheelhouse

The Possibility of Personal Reality Creation

Want clarity? Stop blaming others and make peace with yourself.

Want knowledge? Learn about all belief systems, become accustomed with how people think, and be prepared for your own preconceptions to be wrong.

Want heaven? Believe in a God of empathy and compassion, not punishment.

In the 1970s, Jane Roberts's Seth books presented a metaphysical outlook in which we intrinsically create our own reality.[36] Though clarification on this point is given throughout the series, some take it out of context to this day. The idea that the external world exists *only* as an internalized mental picture is not a useful attitude with which to go through life. Pure solipsism at its worst can be characteristic of mental illness. For one, it abandons *theory of mind*, in which we consider other people to possess independent minds of their own. It is a trait that distinguishes us from the bulk of the animal kingdom.* In singular form, solipsism does not require that we adhere to behavioral standards as outlined by law. Also, any internal perception, such as visual or auditory hallucinations, could be given the same consideration as solid features of the external world. This occasional misinterpretation of the material is an unfortunate consequence sometimes accompanying the positive message of self-empowerment from Roberts's work.

The concept of pure solipsism lies at the extreme opposite of science: that being at the center of the universe as a singular consciousness, rather than unremarkable, even incidental, in the larger scheme. Here, we see two polarities of thought. The propensity of the spiritualist is to seek control of life through unconventional means, whether it is communication with a higher power, or believing oneself to be that higher power. The big picture science provides is based in intellectual and existential humility. Roberts indirectly distinguishes "Sethian philosophy," as it's often referred to, from pure solipsism, with two ideas: that we also create reality collectively,[37] and the "I" that creates reality is not merely the conscious self in the moment.[38]

---

* There are indications theory of mind may exist in some other animals.

Though some of the core concepts Roberts presents fit well with a generalized spiritual framework, she also offers many incidental particulars that do not, such as the existence of humanoid civilizations predating humanity.[39] The suggestion that science is itself a belief system[40] is also at odds with the model. Science holds its own integrity apart from beliefs, and in fact, works by challenging them. If beliefs solely shaped reality, and science was a susceptible belief system in itself, then all of the incorrect theories, assumptions, and superstitions dotting history would have shaped the physical world to meet those expectations. But, in fact, ideas like an earth-centered universe were abandoned precisely because they didn't fit the facts.

Roberts claimed to receive this knowledge from a disincarnated personality named Seth, who seemed to adopt a take it or leave it attitude when it came to believing in his existence. In that spirit, we could choose to believe he is actually communicating through her, or that Seth is a wellspring of ideas from the woman's unconscious, or that it's simply an intentional fabrication in order to sell books. In the interest of a balanced viewpoint, this analysis of the concepts will proceed under the presumption that Seth is a product of Roberts's unconscious mind. The authenticity of the material aside, this creative, and perhaps intuitive, wellspring of ideas provides an explanation that doesn't fly in the face of science. In the generalized spiritual framework, the unconscious mind is the portal to a larger reality in any case, making the difference between Roberts and Seth mere semantics. The alleged method of channeling leads us to the second negative repercussion from Roberts's writings: an inordinate number of people claiming to channel knowledge from spirits, often relating material that sounds suspiciously like Roberts's. Channeling was originally born from the spiritualism movement marking the popularity of séances a century earlier. But instead of communication with dead family members, the modern variety dictates entire treatises on the nature of existence. The problem with claiming one's knowledge comes from a non-physical entity is that it often presents as an unreliable source under any scrutiny.

Another criticism is that even in the event the channeler was actually receiving information from beyond the Earthly realm, their mind might alter the message in accordance with their preconceptions. Hints of this are evident in Roberts's material, such as when Seth speaks of the Christ drama as being significant.[41] Catholicism shaped Jane Roberts's childhood beliefs; if she had instead been raised under the doctrine of Mohammed, Buddha, or Hare Krishna's Swami Prabhupada, would Seth have indicated their significance instead?

Roberts's ideas should not be confused with the *law of attraction*, a similar way of thinking in metaphysical circles. It is supposedly a method of attaining desired goals through visualization and positive affirmations. The distinction between these two approaches is belief. Roberts presents the view that we unconsciously form our reality through our beliefs, which we often label as "facts" until we understand their malleable nature.[42]

To an extent, beliefs do form our picture of reality. Beyond perception, however, *conventional thinking* emphasizes that this influence does not extend to the outside world. This includes events that don't result from our own actions, such as an unexpected financial windfall, natural disaster, or the circumstances surrounding one's birth. The point is that we can imagine an occurrence repeatedly and still not believe it at the core of our convictions. Ordinarily, the mind needs some form of evidence in order to accomplish this feat. Perhaps it is the distinction between preconceptions, and the immutable, physical characteristics of the world that override our expectations, that differentiate between beliefs we can change, and those we cannot with any credible substantiation. For example, an individual entertaining a set of beliefs about good and evil supernatural forces fighting for supremacy over the cosmos might take courses in comparative religion or philosophy and reevaluate their opinion. But if that same person habitually tried to convince neurons in their visual cortex that the midday sky appeared a tangerine shade of orange, they might have less success in changing their beliefs, certainly when it came to convincing others that the perception was factual.

At least in the realm of preconceptions, what would it mean in a philosophical sense if our beliefs about the world and ourselves helped to shape events as easily as manipulating characters on cardboard dioramas? As previously discussed, we obviously do not create our reality directly. Our free will extends to things like motor function and speech, but beyond this, we have no visible control over the world around us. But if we have any sort of presence within a larger reality, a larger personality, then perhaps this could be where a rough draft of a life is planned out in conjunction with the world, similar to the way the subconscious formulates a dream. And with respect to the free will part of the dichotomy, within this rough template might lay a degree of play, the potential for the individual consciousness to control the smaller details. Perhaps the larger personality creates multiple stories of a life, and an individual can come across pivotal points where they unknowingly switch tracks, shaping their own destiny. The dichotomy of control and acceptance is evident here. Very rarely does a person's life unfold as they imagine it will in childhood, or even young adulthood. Unexpected things happen. Opinions and personal tastes change and develop. Acceptance of circumstances can be liberating under certain conditions, especially if one is under the impression a higher power is caring for them. In the purview of the generalized spiritual framework, there is evidently a play between our own will, and a design that is realized even before we were born. Really, that *life template* exists independently of linear time, like a person playing a video game who is independent of any artificial, variable timeline within the game, which can be started anew each time.

From its vantage point outside spacetime, the larger self could view itself as shaping the life while the person is living it. Like an author writing a sort of retroactive biography, the larger self could "go back" and introduce elements into chapter 3 that enables a plot device in chapter 17. The metaphysical author could introduce a character early on, intending to reintroduce it later on, then deciding to remove it altogether. With no walls separating the dichotomy of fixed and mutable, the story could, in effect, never be finished, even as our existence appears reasonably consistent from day to day. Memories of our home, spouse, and a litany of other personal details always seem to match reality.

The multiverse hypothesis has become a fixture in science fiction and how people think about the universe. People often ponder on how their lives could be more preferable had they grown up in different circumstances, or made alternate choices. In a purely imaginary sense, one could access a parallel universe by moving sideways through time, or by moving backwards in time and causing a consequential change in the past, thereby finding an alternate present upon their return. Recalling that matter on subatomic scales is essentially manifested out of probability fields,* it could be argued that from some loftier vantage point, our existence is merely implied. The divisions separating us from our hypothetical doppelgängers in alternate

---

* Though it should be noted that the incorrect attributing of the traits of a "part" to its collective "whole," such as comparing the lack of solidity of atoms to macroscopic structures, is known as a *composition fallacy*.

universes might be as thin as tissue paper. Still, there is no way to exercise this possibility in crossing over to a neighboring reality, except perhaps in our imagination. But we can speculate these alternate tracks could exist side by side in a larger reality exceeding time and space. Perhaps an intrinsic characteristic of this larger personality is a state of superpositioning, like the particle in the double-slit experiment. Like appendages of a many-limbed entity in Hinduism, each alternate could study different sets of lessons, collectively providing the larger self with a sort of meta-analysis of life from a particular starting point.

We can incorporate differently sized rings into our funnel illustration. Numbering the rings at seven works for our purposes, though the number is completely arbitrary. It could have just as easily been five, or one hundred thousand. Here, the number seven holds no mystical value and merely best fits the analogy.

The smallest, bottommost ring represents the handful of seconds commonly recognized as the "now." Moving up the stack vertically, the second, slightly larger ring encompasses the surrounding moments, or hours. The third could be thought of as "the day," and is the only one appearing to fit a discrete quantity. The fourth ring could represent seasonal changes, the fifth, a passage of years, or decades, capturing significant periods in a person's life. The sixth ring embodies the entirety of a life, consisting of everything between life's beginning and its end. Again, these divisions are arbitrary and for the sake of illustration, as we are really talking about a continuous, unbroken system.

From the first ring, we have mobility in the physical world. One can pick up an object on a whim, if they so desire. Beyond this, they enter into mental planning. As the field surrounding the moment increases in scale, the corresponding planning becomes more long-term, and memories, more distant. From these higher rings outside the immediate moment we construct events, consciously and unconsciously.

The seventh and largest ring represents the individual's existence in the larger context beyond life, their greater mind. From here, a life is roughly planned out (possibly multiple lives). At each point, the larger field of activity interacts with the available material of the physical world, shuffling around patterns with ever-increasing complexity. In this respect, the dual aspect of the equal grounds premise is maintained. There is no reason these rings couldn't continue to even greater thresholds of awareness, but we are already dealing with hypotheticals as it is.

This is the ultimate expression of the generalized spiritual framework. Some might think it a bit flaky, or frivolous. The skeptic could conclude it presents the very worst traits of magical thinking, such as the mind's unseen intervention in shaping reality, and they might have a valid point. It could easily be flat-out wrong. The only reasoning behind its candidacy for pairing *as a conditional hypothetical* with science, under the umbrella of the equal grounds premise, is its consistency. All things being equal, consistency looks better than inconsistency, but this does not make the framework's veracity irreproachable by any means. Science works in completely opposite ways. Though patterns in nature can be predictable, conclusions based on mere conjecture or a common sense approach don't work. The truth typically lies around invisible corners, found and confirmed through testing under controlled conditions. Religion tries to recreate these twists and turns with allegories involving humans and deities. But even at the height of Greek civilization, the existence of the gods and goddesses, or stories of the trials they put mere mortals through, was never subject to verification. The appeal in believing in them was that people could relate to these higher beings, since they were invested with the same fallibilities and propensity for rash action. The operating assumption at the time was that these deities were not superior in any moral sense. More importantly, these gods and goddesses were the direct expressions of human traits, not individuals per se. They existed independently of our free will.

Some practitioners of Western religion especially might take issue with the formulation of the framework proposed here, pointing to a God in heaven and humans on Earth as the simplest configuration of ideas. But this leaves us with two things, not one. In contrast, the dichotomy of the equal grounds premise is presented as two views on the same ultimate reality.

Many Eastern religions portray the soul as evolving, eventually escaping the cycle of the material world. But if the perception of linear time doesn't apply in this fashion, couldn't it be argued that we, in a sense, are already there?

The generalized spiritual framework is a process of consciousness repeated at a range of scales, in the midst of a dichotomy posed by the equal grounds premise. One half of the dichotomy consists of a realist view of a shared, material universe outside ourselves, in which we are incidental. In the other half, we each lie within a larger reality, through which we ultimately extend ad infinitum. This hypothetical framework of spirituality is complimentary to science *precisely because* it is unstructured. The premise that science and generalized spirituality are in equal standing echoes the model of free will versus determinism, where instead of arrows exclusively pointing inward or outward, both are correct, without contradiction. This third, porous model, where a timeless environment intersects a temporal one, is a concept referred to earlier as attunement. It is a concept embodied by a universe that originates and develops randomly, while being synchronous with a larger realm, which is purposeful. This could be applied to the processes that keep the body functioning. Because of random collisions between molecules called Brownian motion, a molecule can meander aimlessly through a cell's cytoplasm until it winds up in a place where it can be of use. Amidst the disarray, there is enough order to keep the systems functioning. One could argue the purpose inherent in the larger realm would blanket both systems, making the physical universe purposeful as well. But what intrinsically cannot be scientifically measured creates the distinction between the two systems. The appearance of purposeful design to the universe is not the same as empirical evidence, so spiritual matters must respectfully stay clear of science, resulting in what might appear as a randomly unfolding universe.

But on the spiritual side of the dichotomy, the generalized framework strongly implies the conscious mind manipulates the physical environment in the moment, while deeper layers of the mind manipulate matter on a larger scale, in the formation of events. Deeper still, the larger personality, or soul, creates the picture of the life.

The equal grounds premise could be thought of as a nutshell containing the two diametrically opposed, yet complimentary, schools of thought.

An obvious issue pertaining to the idea of reality creation is that it would require a concerted effort between all individuals involved. One possibility is a negotiation of sorts, in which those people are forced to compromise on planned events, much as they do in conscious life. Another possibility is that the existence of a multiverse allows each individual to essentially create his or her own timeline with respect to the wishes of others. Without straying too far from the central tenet of keeping speculation at a minimum, we might attribute elements of both to the process.

Another question pertains to the persistence of the physical world even if there was no conscious life. But if consciousness were a fundamental aspect of the universe, the matter comprising the physical stuff of the universe would hold up under its own integrity, without the need for an independent creator.

A positive impact of the reality creation idea is a refusal to be a victim. A negative ramification of this position is that sometimes there *are* victims. Children and women are abused. Otherwise peaceful regions are terrorized by war. People endure starvation and disease. There *is* a place for outrage, a call for change, rather than acceptance. It seems an unbalanced proposition to sacrifice our humanity for a convenient philosophy. But more than that, it is hard to believe a soul would place one of its beloved personalities into a situation of torment.

Theodicies are arguments that try to explain how God allows suffering. In bringing the subject into this venue, we are really just switching the labels of a higher power from God, to the more intermediary power of the larger personality. Perhaps the difference lies in the fact that though God may know our hearts, He or She is ultimately apart from us. God's wisdom, or divine plan, remains a mystery. In the case of the larger personality, it is arguably a larger aspect of that person placing themselves in dire circumstances. In the case the hapless individual is what we truly identify with as a victim, such as a child, it seems reprehensible to consider their suffering as in any way self-inflicted. Due to this ethical entanglement, some of whom find this belief system otherwise appealing might consider it best to focus on themselves alone in this respect.

Playing with causality in this model, we could just as easily say the world tends to reflect what an individual believes, as if creating justifications. This would mean the person who believes crime and corruption are everywhere is more likely to be presented with examples of this, even beyond information sources they deliberately seek out. In contrast, the individual who believes in the goodness of people encounters the genuinely amiable sort more often. Likely untestable because of its scope, this concept falls under the purview of judgment according to personal experience.

Another possible permutation is that some use rituals, invocations, or other forms of magical thinking to provide themselves with a sense of power over events they unconsciously know are already being manifested, further reinforcing their belief system in the process. The flip side of this is using elements such as tarot cards or tea leaves to bring imminent manifestations to conscious attention, a sort of premonition by proxy.

Whereas some might assume this philosophy functions as the ultimate evasion from responsibility, it is quite the opposite. It's not about getting what you want, which implies control. It's about understanding your lot in life, and finding opportunities for growth that may lie hidden. It's acknowledging the possibility that you get many chances to view life from different vantage points in the realm of human experience.

On the one hand, we are galaxy-sized enormities of consciousness with hands in countless projects, shaping worlds like clay on a pottery wheel. Life is a mission. When we are done, we go home. But in the meantime, there are people to connect with, subjects to learn. Sometimes we seem to abandon one path only to be presented with another. Something is always gained. No pressure.

On the other hand, we are molecules come together into lively configurations. Beneath a sky laden with stars, this is where our adventure begins, using our still-developing faculties with a hint of imagination to uncover this expanse around us. We carve out a niche in which to develop our personalities and better ourselves, and if we are very fortunate, we are able to help others. Life is freeform. Much of it, we make up as we go, and nothing is wasted as long as we learn from our mistakes. It's not supposed to be perfect. No pressure.

Imagine taking responsibility for your entire life as your personal story, even the circumstances of your birth. Making it your own. Taking pride in even the dark spots, the rough patches, the experience gained. Viewing yourself as a character in a story, becoming more in the process. Peering in from outside of life, death loses its sting. Not applying blame to anyone or anything. Some may think this unhealthy or delusional. I think it shows incredible maturity. Imagine a world full of such people, where accountability was embraced, but blame was nowhere to be had.

EIGHT

Sunset

A Cautionary Tale

It's estimated there have been about 100 billion people in the world, ever.

All of them entertained their theories of the world, which spirits to pay homage to, what peoples and governments were responsible for life being what it was at the worst of times.

We just got here, yet the finger pointing remains, like it's new. Look around you at the world, but without applying blame. Then you see it as it actually is, at least on the surface: a carnival of confusion and mixed ideologies.

But in the midst of this, there is something more, a process of learning that sticks with subsequent generations. This, above all else, we must preserve.

The late, eminent astrophysicist Carl Sagan wrote, "We live in a society exquisitely dependent on science and technology, in which hardly anyone knows anything about science and technology."[43] His landmark educational miniseries *Cosmos*, and book of the same name, took the world by storm. He demonstrated an uncommon ability to communicate scientific concepts to the novice mind. Though it is evident by his requirement for empirical evidence that he would *not* endorse the approach forwarded by this book, Dr. Sagan seemed to possess a unique brand of spirituality in grasping the sheer scale of where we are, and capturing the breathtaking beauty within it, which he then tried to impart to others. Perhaps most importantly, he impressed upon many the need for tireless skepticism. He understood how potentially perilous a society uneducated in science could be, relating that science as way of thinking could be employed in various areas of life.[44]

The philosophy promoted in this book has ambiguity deliberately built into it. It is proposed as an alternative for those who hold and admire science as a tool to better humanity's course, but also feel the big picture may go beyond the capabilities of scientific methodology.

Much has happened to metaphysical ideas since philosophical figures like Descartes and his deductive reasoning to prove he exists as a thinking being. In common usage, the word metaphysics is heavily associated with pseudoscience. Somewhat divorced from philosophy, its popular usage calls for little debate using logic, only a search for the next cache of ideas that can rake in income through books and workshops.

If we can concur that maintaining our survival as a species constitutes a moral obligation, and that cooperation and sharing of ideas between human beings has facilitated our survival to this point, then we have a moral duty to promote truth. If there is *metaphysical* truth to be had, we are obligated to get it right, and understanding science provides a backdrop for that bigger picture. Pseudoscience has made asking the big questions of philosophy unfashionable. Its misrepresentation of science has only served to make metaphysical speculation a subject of prejudice in the scientific community. Purveyors of such misrepresentation should be aware of this and the consequential damage they are doing to the cause of human knowledge, while the scientific mind should be aware of the tendency to dismiss spiritual-based ideas out of hand so that they can determine if these biases exist in their own thinking.

The world is caught up in an epidemic of science denial. Anti-vaccination proponents and climate change skeptics are taking our species toward the edge of an abyss. The rational course is to accept the findings of the scientific community on any issue concerning the material world. If the position of the scientific community changes, one should follow this by adopting the new view. This reasoning is based on the fact that experts in their fields base their conclusions on a plethora of studies conducted with careful safeguards, data the average individual cannot easily obtain or absorb. Sometimes science changes its course, and this is natural. It is similar to how our own preconceptions about the world change as we grow older and learn more. The perception that the bulk of scientific research is somehow "faked" for economic or political agendas is absurd. We know this because science *does* move forward, and our world *is* significantly different than a century, or even decades past. The conclusion we can draw from this is that *science works,* and next to the complex process of experimentation and peer review, the opinion of the layman is effectively guesswork.

Pseudoscience advocates share in the responsibility for science denial, with claims of positive thinking and "natural" cures to combat illness. Conspiracy theorists are also complicit, blanketing society in a dark, paranoid worldview displaying a lack of faith in human nature. These two factors together culminate in some of the most peculiar beliefs. Possibly the oddest groups to emerge are those claiming the Earth to be flat. Most who claim to believe it are just trolling the internet for fun, but a small fraction among them actually seems to believe there is a massive cover-up hiding the shape of the Earth. Though relatively harmless as compared to some other groups, the striking heretical attitude toward science makes it a perfect example for examination. To illustrate the contrast with conventional thinking, the following is a fictional tale of flat Earth:

It is the year 2167, year 84 of the New Renaissance. In the past several decades, the Institute of Earth Science (IES) has mapped out the entire surface of the Earth with airships out to the surrounding ice wall. Were someone adventurous enough and found a clear path along the wall, it is said one could circle the Earth on horseback in as little as a year.

I was but a youngster when the Sun was first explored. A white-hot stone, it slowly crawls across the sky in circular fashion under its own power. It is said the airship could only venture as close as a few miles before the sap helping to hold the observation deck together began to melt away. Under the tutelage of the magistrate and the Royal House, many such expeditions were launched. Word has it the celestial dome itself was touched by a lieutenant in the exploratory guard, describing the star-strewn surface as "something Michelangelo himself might have painted on God's Cathedral."

Through the fissures in the ice wall, a vast open space beneath the Earth was revealed, a featureless stone slab spanning the underside of the world, as far as the eye could see. Below this lies a great nothingness, which swallowed an unwary aircrew without warning (God save those fifteen souls). It was scientifically determined that this endless well of nothingness was responsible for the pull-down force, which keeps things stuck to the Earth.

The wandering lights against the sky are said to be spirits that watch over the Royal House, though some say they existed even before then. They bear ancient names like Jupiter *and* Mars. *The banning of spyglass technology ensures there are no uneducated falsehoods about the heavens spreading in hushed whispers, ever since it was discovered that imagination filled in details that weren't actually present in the magnification. The mind plays tricks (especially at my age).*

117

The moon is a complex lighthouse contraption capable of casting shadows upon itself. For a time, in childhood, I wondered if perhaps great sky beings once used the moon as a lighthouse to guide their way. But now with the benefit of science, I know these frivolous daydreams are fantasy alone, as the IES has determined there is nothing beyond the firmament surrounding our universe, all 700,000 square miles of it. A staggering number, to be sure.

Ah, to ride upon a great dirigible, viewing all the world from on high, but alas, it is forbidden. Only the specially trained are allowed to venture to the edge of the world, for one wrong move could plummet one to certain death. Those who try are never seen again.

And so, I sit here amidst these cold, dead antiquities of the deceitful old age, 'lectronics and such, jotting down my observations for posterity like the foolish old man that I am.

— Harold the Younger,
Royal Historian

Then there's the alternative view:

The Sun is a star, very near to us.

Anyone who has ever looked up at the night sky unfettered by city lights knows how breathtaking it is. The light from our home star obscures the surrounding panorama, but it is always there. The bright patch we see stretching across the sky is the disk of our galaxy, the Milky Way, seen edge-on from inside it. And all of these countless stars we can see fit within a small portion of the galaxy, our neighbors in a galactic suburb. The rest are too far away or obscured by dust. There are about 400 billion stars in our galaxy, at least a couple of trillion other galaxies. That's a lot of suns, a lot of worlds.

The Earth is round. This is because bits and pieces of rocky dust collect together from their gravity, roughly forming a sphere over time. Gravity works the same everywhere in the universe. Once you understand these basic principles, a flat Earth simply doesn't make sense. Space itself is curved, into the fourth dimension of time. This curvature, according to general relativity, illustrates gravity as a depression in the fabric of space that nearby objects roll into (like a bowling ball resting on a mattress). It seems some of the most introspective ideas involve realizing some larger portion of reality that extends beyond our view, physically or conceptually.

Perhaps it's natural to expect the Earth to be flat at first glance. It's what the eyes extrapolate. In contrast, it may be difficult to conceptualize such a massive scale where gravity would pull each point toward the center, a matter of scale where unfamiliar laws of nature take shape. After all, our brains are designed for the savanna, and Paleolithic humans rarely needed to conceptualize anything beyond the distant horizon.

There is a stark contrast between the two ideas of how our universe is designed. The fictional historian's account in the beginning tells us a few things. Played out in some detail, a flat Earth seems even a bit more silly than one might expect, maybe even to those who subscribe to it. How could there be a universe the size of the Earth? What else is there? Is there no potential for further discovery? Also, as some may have noticed, the tale is told as if the presiding establishment isn't quite disclosing the truth of the world to its people. More than that, they seem to be keeping them from it. There are no special conditions or requirements for a government to deceive its citizens. The only way to limit the possibility of this happening is to ensure knowledge of the world is made freely available to everyone. The alternative to this is that knowledge is only accessible to an elite class or organization.

Older generations may recall having to go to the library to look up information. Now the accumulated knowledge of the species is available at one's fingertips. A classroom once had the nearly exclusive distinction as a place of learning, but now everyone with an online video is a teacher, especially in the minds of impressionable younger generations who don't remember a time before technology. The distinctions have become blurred, and there may simply be too many conflicting information sources to make sense of them.

In this event, in the apparent absence of definitive "facts," a person might very well take on whatever belief system suits their beliefs and personality type. It could be a worldview of paranoia and distrust, or rebelliousness. What is known to science could fill entire libraries, knowledge gained over many centuries of human exploration into how the world works.

The beauty of science is its consistency, its brutal honesty. It's what has shaped the industry and technology of the world we live in. But it might be intimidating for some. Flat Earth and other science denial conspiracy theories attempting to debunk science as fraudulent and claiming a global government cover-up have little content in comparison. It might simply be easier to believe for this reason. And if a person wants to understand the world they're in and what lay beyond, if they really are hard-pressed to find truth, they will probably feel compelled to look at a variety of belief systems and not settle with the first thing to come along.

It's likely that most flat Earthers don't actually care about the nature of the universe. Without the perspective that learning the history of science gives, flat Earth may be viewed by some as a new and trending, cutting-edge fantasy. To use a fashion expression, it is "the new black." Science does not discourage looking over pseudoscience material, when, in fact, it may be a necessary courtesy if future debate is anticipated. In contrast, flat Earth sources often discourage learning science, using such descriptives as "indoctrination" and "brainwashing."

But the spirit of science is anything but. Beyond the human frailties we all have, if one scientist shows another scientist evidence their theory is wrong, they must abandon it, no matter how much they like it personally.[45] And when an experiment gives unexpected results, it can be exciting because the experimenter found out something new even if it doesn't support their idea. The aim of the scientist is not to prove themselves right, but to find the truth, regardless of what it might be.

And let's dispel the misconception that science is like a secret code consisting of formulas plastered across a chalkboard. Though mathematics is an invaluable tool to prove or calculate something, the concepts are easy to grasp if explained well. Spectroscopy is an excellent example. Atoms play with light, and this is a cornerstone of the physical sciences. Every kind of atom and molecule absorbs or reflects light at a different frequency, resulting in a distinctive signature, unique as a fingerprint. This is generally the same technique crime scene investigators use to determine compositions of materials. Astronomers use this technique to understand what distant stars are made of, but simple spectrophotometers can be found in college classrooms. And a college student in the physical sciences can do the math and see that objects in the universe move just as science claims, and fitting observation. There are even programs and phone apps that allow viewing of any part of the solar system, at any point in past or future, from any vantage point.

The issue is the future, as impressionable, younger generations see posts and follow threads on social media with the impression that theories contradictory to science are in equal standing, or nearly so, which is a ridiculous assertion. This is especially true when counting the proven products of science in the modern world. Just contributions from medical science alone have greatly improved the quality of life worldwide. Weighed against the nonexistent contributions of pseudoscience, it becomes clear the latter has actually hindered our stride into the future.

Some conspiracy theories don't try to debunk science itself, but rather milestones humanity has achieved, which brings us to Apollo deniers. Conspiracy theory can have its allure, and some may quickly conclude in this day and age of computer-generated images that constructing a fairly realistic soundstage in that era would have been more feasible than going through the trouble of actually sending astronauts to the moon, but not if you really take a moment to think about it. Let's step back and look at this rationally.

First, there's the massive amount of planning that went into the endeavor, many years of sifting through designs. It could be argued that putting together such an elaborate illusion would be almost as difficult and costly as trying to reach the moon. So, why weave such a fiction involving the secrecy of thousands of individuals when we could just try to send astronauts to the moon?

This brings us to those who claim the moon program was "well-intentioned to begin with, but NASA was unable to make it work." Millions throughout the world saw the Saturn V rocket launch after the astronauts boarded. Unless you believe the entire space program was faked, there is no disputing this fact. Once the astronauts in their capsule were out of the atmosphere and away from the majority of Earth's gravity, the journey to the moon would be a comparatively easy sail. They would simply have to slow down on approach for landing.

Again, if they were capable of getting this far, why not just do it? Getting the astronauts and payload off the Earth was the hard part. Any physicist can attest to this. When we include the command module and lunar excursion module built to design and fitted onto the nose of the Saturn V booster rocket, it's a bit analogous to having a house built to precise specifications over many years' time, then deciding the project is too much work when it comes time to move in the furniture. It's simply not reasonable.

Also, if a hoax were perpetrated to facilitate political advantages gained by such an agenda, then what has changed since to curtail this practice? Russia (formerly the Soviet Union), Japan, India, and China have all sent probes to the moon, yet none of these countries claim to have set foot there. Furthermore, no one claims to have sent astronauts to Mars, even though in the late 1960s onward it seemed like the next logical step after the moon missions. During this time, speculation abounded that there would be bases on the moon by the turn of the millennium. If there were a great potential for hoaxes in the space program and much clout to be gained in the international community, most especially in these days of realistic computer special effects, someone would have surely snatched up the opportunity. But India does not claim to have planted its flag next to a Martian Habitat. Brazil does not post pictures of the Amazon Rainforest purporting them as a colony on the Jovian moon of Europa.

One reason is that scientists keep each other honest. If a researcher makes a claim that seems outside their capabilities, the scientific community at large calls them out. The other reason is that science itself is based on an honest representation of the facts. This is not always the case because of government or corporate intellectual property concerns and nondisclosure agreements, not to mention the occasional case of falsified data for personal gain, but openness and reproducible results is the heart of what science is about. This process of building verifiable ideas atop each other is actually what got us this far in an age of medicine and technological convenience. A history of science tells volumes about its methods.

The flat Earth tale may not be simply fiction, but a window on the future, because we've walked backwards before. Scientific experimentation had begun accumulating facts about the natural world when it was knocked out of favor, and shortly thereafter we emerged into the Dark Ages.

The Library of Alexandria was the greatest repository of knowledge in the ancient world. Docked ships were searched for scrolls, which were copied to the library's shelves and then returned. They knew the world was round a thousand years before Columbus. Most of this knowledge was lost when it was burned down by a mob of religious zealots. This, in part, signaled the beginning of the Dark Ages. And when the Renaissance took the reins centuries ago, the fundamentals of scientific method returned.[46] And here we are, questioning science once again, which in principle is fine if you take the time to find out what it is.

It's difficult to imagine a return to that era where assumption and superstition are the rule. Where disease runs rampant and the ability to read belongs to an elite few, so they can tell the people their exclusive interpretation on what life in the universe is.

The reason behind the story is the possibility that civilization could be set back by a natural disaster or other cataclysm. Of all the things that could conceivably upset our way of life, some say we are overdue. The Carrington Event of 1859 was a massive solar storm that burned out telegraph wires in the United States and Europe. If an electromagnetic pulse (EMP) of this strength hit the Earth today, there is little doubt a large number of power grids in the world would fail permanently, with no large replacement transformers on hand. These monstrous pieces of machinery are only produced in Germany and South Korea, and can take up to two years to build. When they are brought across the ocean, bridges must be reinforced and roads widened to deliver them to their final location.[47] If much of the world is plunged into darkness, and in the ensuing chaos, financial markets collapse while governments falter, replacing burned out transformers may not realistically be an implementable contingency plan for years or longer.

A nuclear exchange between major world powers would be preceded by high-altitude EMP blasts, having much the same effect, though it goes without saying that far greater problems would directly follow from casualties on an unparalleled scale. Thousands of these weapons are kept on hair-trigger alert, and more countries are added to the roster of nuclear-armed states with the passing of each decade. There have been a truly frightening number of close calls since the nuclear age began, and the inadvertent nature of these suggest that if a nuclear war were to happen, it would probably be as a result of an accident or misunderstanding. The idea known as *mutually assured destruction* (MAD) presents the case that launching against a foe would be suicide, as a retaliatory launch would immediately follow. This is often touted as the reason why a nuclear war is impossible. But MAD is only a deterrent in intentional, preemptive first strikes, not accidental launches. Reason dictates we are faced with two options: find a way to mutually disarm and prevent nuclear proliferation in other nations, or these instruments of massive destruction will eventually be used.

With basic survival in play following such a disaster, it is not unreasonable that some figures would step up to choose a direction for humanity to take. Would we take the pause as an opportunity to reassess ourselves as a species, take what we know works, that which improves the quality of life, while electing to work on ourselves? Or would we go backwards once again, accepting baseless "facts" rooted in assumption, a feudal society which rewrites history such that our long strides are forgotten. And we would have to go through it all over again. All that will have been time wasted. Again. Just imagine where we'd be if we had moved forward all along.

We sit on the verge of an exciting time where science has made so much possible. But if society takes a significant wrong turn headlong into distrust and paranoia, we may actually be on a precipice.

Where we go from here depends mostly on ordinary people like you and I. Learn all that you can. Discriminate information by its source and evidence, but also its plausibility. Most importantly, be aware of why a particular belief system may appeal to you personally, and be prepared to question it further, or cast it aside if the motivation is confirmation of a personal worldview, and not the pursuit of knowledge. The same elements you feel exist in your life will color your worldview. If you see lies and deceit around you, that could easily be projected onto everything considered to be mainstream knowledge. If you believe in the goodness of the human spirit, its curiosity maintained by self-honesty and accountability to the human species, you might see this as well. Be aware of how your own mind works as well as how other people think.

Then teach. Just teach.

NINE

Tearing Away the Sky

Speculations on Humanity's Best Destiny

After dozens of centuries and countless contributing scholars, we finally have the collective knowledge of human civilization in one place, easily accessible by anyone. Let history testify we used it to better ourselves and reach the stars.

The middle of the last century was an interesting time. We found ways to vanquish the dreaded germs that had plagued us throughout history. We preventively put antibiotics in our mouthwash, toothpastes, and deodorant (yes, they did this). With our developed brains, we were the only thinking, conscious beings, a miracle of evolution in a Darwinistic world. We fostered dreams of going into space. With our newly found atomic power, our rocket ships would colonize the stars, and we would proudly plant our flag as supreme masters of the cosmos . . .

Except it didn't turn out that way. It wasn't exactly Darwin's dog-eat-dog world after all, but cooperation at least as much as a competition, full of symbiotic relationships. We didn't see the big picture.

The dictum of *kill all germs* backfired. We did not understand their versatility, evolving a thousand times faster than we do. We now pay the price, scrambling to find new classes of antibiotics to fight hardy, resistant strains, the old biological miracles of medicine virtually useless. As it turns out, our bodily ecosystems are great zoos of these tiny creatures, assisting our physiology. In fact, it has recently been discovered that the bulk of genetic material in our bodies belongs to them.

Animals are thinking and feeling creatures, it turns out. Not quite like we humans, but they do feel pain and suffering, once thought to be instinctive reactions. They can figure out puzzles, and it seems some possess a theory of mind.

Though nuclear power is invaluable to our growing population, the thermonuclear successor to the atom bomb holds our world hostage.

And the cosmos turned out to be a much more structured and stranger place than we ever gave it credit for.

Regardless of whether a larger reality exists or not, the big picture of the universe almost certainly involves the development of life elsewhere. The difficulty with conjecture is we have only one example to extrapolate the possibilities from: the Earth itself. From science, we know what materials are most likely to be utilized in nature's endeavors. Carbon is highly versatile, for example, and liquid water holds advantageous properties. In speculating beyond points of basic chemistry, there is a temptation in science fiction to extend the characteristics of human beings as models for intelligent, alien life even further, such as greed, avarice, and a push for colonization. If we are to make these distinctions, the evaluation should fully represent who we are. While many negative points of human nature continue to exist, we have made notable strides.

Nations still invade other nations, but usually require a pretext to do so. Generally speaking, the world populace expects that sovereignty be respected. This is a far cry from the ancient world, where walled cities frequently fell under siege, the inhabitants killed or sold into slavery.

Slavery itself was once thought be a fact of life, and was never questioned until recently in history. Now it is nearly abolished.

Representing half the world's population, the veil of oppression has been lifted for women in most countries, freeing them to become doctors, lawyers, scientists, and politicians, to name a few, roles traditionally held by men.

We've enslaved entire species for food consumption. Though it is not a majority, there is a calling from many animal rights advocates that the food industry give these animals some quality of life and minimize suffering. This is also the case for medical and cosmetic testing industries. Animal abuse laws with stiff penalties are becoming more prevalent. This is especially notable if a mentally advanced alien race is trying to distinguish if we are conscious, intelligent creatures.

One can argue that we *do* evolve as a species, intellectually and emotionally. It has been a slow process, but in most sectors of the world, we are far different than we were a couple of centuries ago, certainly millennia. And the process is advancing exponentially as ideas and cultures are shared across the world without impediment. The concept of conquering new worlds for resources may simply be a dated one, perhaps not even applicable considering all we don't know about the larger universe.

Another point is that aliens that have mastered interstellar travel have possibly been in equivalent places to where we have been, where we are now, and shall be in the future. Along such a path, it would have been difficult to not see a cooperative universe, or at least something that resembles one.

In the midst of speculation, we are just dealing with possibilities. Some might argue that it would be unfair to take the worst of humanity and apply it to another species, but leave the rest. A comparison should be whole and balanced. Even then, we could not fairly base sentient aliens capable of star travel on where we have been, but who we will become.

It appears in a public place. Not so much out of nothingness, but the slow realization dawns of it simply being there as wayfarers shake their heads in befuddlement. The winding staircase leads to a doorway. Changing perspective reveals an environment beyond the portal where there should only be empty air. Surely it is some kind of trick. Some might look around for a magician or hidden cameras, smiling with uncertainty. A few might dial 911 not knowing quite what to say, or gaze in disbelief while holding up their smartphones. How many would briskly walk by, trying to push the absurdity out of mind? How many would adventurously tread up those stairs? And how many wouldn't register it at all, the supernatural event falling into a mental blind spot.

We often imagine aliens arriving in metallic ships. But it could be said we have an infant's view of the universe and its inner workings. If they surpass us to this degree, the everyday set of symbols with which we are familiar would provide forms for a genuine first contact. If it were not a random location, they probably would not arrive on the White House lawn or in Red Square. If they knew enough about us to determine where our leadership resided, it's likely these aliens would make their debut on the grounds of a prestigious university, or NASA's Jet Propulsion Laboratory, seeking knowledgeable minds less likely to perceive them as a threat and react out of fear.

The bridge between worlds could be an absurdity suddenly appearing, or something completely innocuous. It could even be *inserted* into our reality, as say, an extra apartment building or place of business that wasn't there before, but through some overwriting technique, no one is the wiser. Such a transcendent being could merely pose as a kiosk or food truck operator, watching the world go by, observing people's behavior to satisfy curiosities of agencies beyond our imaginings.

If aliens a century more advanced than us visited Earth, we would be hard-pressed to offer any kind of resistance. In the case of aliens a thousand or million years more advanced than us, again, there would be no ships, at least as we understand the term. They could simply appear with seemingly godlike powers and we would be completely powerless to alter their course of purpose.

In either case, our best chance would be communication, expressing our sentience, which would likely be dwarfed by theirs. But our species would both likely share similar stories of rising up from a primordial soup under their respective stars, and perhaps this primal genesis would represent a fundamental common ground between us. Or, the universe could be brimming with AI, the organics that develop them, shortly after disappearing from sight. These new, electric fauna might view their ancient creators with neither reverence nor contempt, but with the same nonchalance with which we regard the single-celled eukaryotes we emerged from. Perhaps this artificial life would continue to develop itself, making copies and improving upon each generation. Thinking, feeling, super-intelligent behemoths could fill the expanse of night, with a mastery of space, and an appreciation for knowledge, even beauty. With regards to present day Earth, it's conceivable they might make first contact with the emerging intelligence they perceive, the internet, regarding we humans as little more than evolution-facilitating enzymes.

But where are the aliens of simpler times and comparable technological development, the ones like us? The ones that perhaps see our star in their night sky and wonder about the possibilities? It's turning out to look like there are plenty of Earth-like planets out there. So, why is it so quiet? It could just be a matter of timing.

Keep in mind, we've only had radio capability for close to a century, and that's a speck of time considering the lifetime of our world. It is quite possible intelligent species emerge and wink out just as quickly. This could be due to planetary catastrophe,* contagion, or self-destruction (as in the famous Drake equation). Intelligent species are likely to create better methods of communication than radio signals at some point, or tweak them in ways that make them likewise undetectable to us. Or species could *ascend* for lack of a better term, evolving to work with non-physical information sets not available to us. Such beings could overlook the physical realm from an

---

* Geological records show that Earth has seen five extinction events that we know of.

adjacent space using technology far beyond us, perhaps even being *more conscious* than we are. While revolving around the Sun in accordance with Newtonian physics, Earth could simultaneously serve as a showpiece in a sort of metaphysical museum. The likelihood that some semblance of this is true depends largely on the consciousness question.

First broadcasts would probably not be aimed at contacting other worlds if we were any indication, but incidentals like sporting events, game shows, and fictional dramas. Guessing at merely a handful of intelligent species within a hundred light years over the millennia, a few shells of radio broadcasts, traveling at the speed of light, may have missed our technological era entirely. The Caesars may have missed out on alien soap operas. Another one could have missed during the Dark Ages or the Renaissance. One *civilization broadcast* could be heading our way now, though that species may no longer be with us when it arrives. Imagine how our civilization would be dedicated to understanding these cosmic cousins, their language and culture, which would inevitably shape ours.

In response to recent public disclosures by the United States Navy on the subject of UFO encounters,[48] it's difficult to claim UFOs don't exist, but it might be premature to claim to know exactly what they are. This is because nature likes to surprise us by detouring around obvious explanations with more complex answers.

Take the Salem witch trials, for instance, wherein what appeared to be a clear-cut case of demonic possession was most likely a group of girls hallucinating from ergot fungus that had grown on the rye that was made into bread. But in that time, virtually nothing was known about biochemistry, and evil spirits made sense in the strict Calvinist doctrine the pilgrims lived by. In this technological age, society wonders about life elsewhere in the universe. An archetypal equivalent of evolved humanoid beings in metal ships is the easiest explanation, but there is still so much we don't know.

It would seem the wacky behaviors and shapes UFOs exhibit are connected with some form of consciousness, either our own, or perhaps mixed with that of another agency. Though it does seem unlikely for it all to be natural phenomena and weather balloons, we can't rule out the metaphorical ergot: the possibility that the experiences aren't hallucinations per se, but a part of a larger system enmeshed with perceptions that we don't yet fully understand. Emissaries and symbols from the heavens have taken forms of everything from a burning bush to blimps. Whatever the ergot is, it seems to keep up with our technological development, if not our culture.

That's not to say people are hallucinating as though something isn't actually there, as much as materializing information out of our minds somehow into the outside world, thus becoming real for all intents and purposes. In a boundless information universe, these events could be something else taking the shape of our thoughts, a dimly aware, but ever-present cosmic consciousness. This could constitute a sort of glitch in the hypothetical program underpinning and knitting together a shared reality, or it could be a projection of archetypes from the collective unconscious.

We've known about the strangeness of the quantum world and how it may subtly entangle with consciousness for about a century now. Our shared reality is measurable, but perhaps fundamentally suspect as well. Maybe in the next century we will find out just how deeply the rabbit hole goes. We are biological machines, made of the same stuff as all the rest, in complex configurations. The universe views itself through our eyes. Perhaps the universe also dreams.

A Paleolithic woman watches the dull flicker of the fire dance across the cave wall. It kept the animals from the mouth of the cave so she could rest in reasonable safety near the others. She often watched the points of light appear outside until darkness fell and it was necessary to come inside. There were no words for the tiny lights in the sky. She sometimes wondered if the others saw them at all. Her name a monosyllabic grunt, we'll simply call her Gloria. Wrapping herself in an animal skin, she closes her eyes and falls peacefully to sleep.

Gloria awakens in the middle of New York's Manhattan, Times Square, to be precise. The relative quiet of the cave life sharply contrasts with the din of pedestrian footfalls on asphalt moving in herds at crosswalks, and conversations spoken into empty air. Large, shiny animals with headlights for eyes and grills for mouths growl and hum, the spirits of people trapped inside. All the while, the siren wail of a great predator echoes from far away, perhaps warding others away from its kill.

The people all about wear skins of strange colors, many staring at the palms of their hands, while canyon walls stretched to the sky, a thousand orange eyes looking down on her, reflections of the rising sun. Terrified, Gloria curls into a fetal position while onlookers crowd around, holding small, unfamiliar objects in the air, pointed right at her . . .

While Gloria's brain from a hundred thousand years ago is nearly identical to ours in nearly all respects, the symbols of the modern world have almost no links to items in the familiar Paleolithic era. Natural landscape, vegetation, and animals are largely replaced in this case with skyscrapers, traffic, blinking lights, and smartphones. Without familiar meanings with which to commit these observations to memory, what she was seeing would present as a collection of associative blurs. Had Gloria returned to her time, the experience she relayed to those of her tribe would be limited to familiar descriptive words and concepts, but also by the vagueness of what she'd seen being quickly overwritten as her mind attempted to hold onto it using things already known to her. Some of the earlier stone tools would likely exist in her world, as well as the makings of the fire that protects and cooks, but the largest numbers used described the amount of food stores or animal skins. Next to caves, primitive dwellings made from sticks and mud may as well have been science fiction.

What would travelers from the present experience a thousand, or even ten thousand years from now? Accounting for the technology curve, as well as the culmination of ideas and cultures from around the world, such a leap might be as profound a change as Gloria encountered.

Information was once shared by word of mouth in stories. Then writing presented a way for ideas to reach out to future generations. The advancement in information storage and sharing in recent decades has been computers and telecommunications. The capacities and delivery speeds are leaps and bounds beyond anything our ancestors of centuries past knew, perfectly incomprehensible in Gloria's time. Science fiction would often have future generations aboard metallic ships, battling alien species while befriending others and colonizing worlds. But are we still susceptible to casting the future of cultural/technological transformation into familiar constructs? The push-button technology in early science fiction was easily surpassed by later generations of the genre, even though it represented the future. Perhaps this, more than anything, demonstrates not only how quickly our technology outpaces our expectations, but also just how alien the distant future might look to us next to our preconceptions. Our travelers into that distant future might find a planet seemingly untouched by an intelligent species, with no signs of previous civilization. Where did all the people go? And if there had been a global cataclysm of some kind, where are the remnants of structures and products of industry?

Author Arthur C. Clarke is perhaps the best known science fiction writer of the past century. He has demonstrated an uncanny foresight of future technological development, such as the communications satellites that make our modern civilization possible. One theme that is prevalent in his novels is the idea that great agencies of consciousness exist independently of space and time. These god-like gestalts are not deities, but intelligent creatures that seemed to have climbed the ladder of development beyond the physical world that we perceive. Whether it is the monolith of *2001: A Space Odyssey*,[49] the Grand Galactic farming interstellar gas clouds to promote star growth in *The Last Theorem* (with Frederik Pohl),[50] or an unknown agency chopping the world into different time regions for likewise unknown purposes in *Time's Eye* (with Stephen Baxter),[51] these embassies of larger consciousness are deeply immersed in cosmic tasks far beyond our comprehension.

It's possible that when a technologically advanced civilization sufficiently understands the universe first and foremost as an information picture, they are subsequently able to manipulate it in ways we can barely imagine. Perhaps this is why it is so quiet out there, other civilizations communicating, even interacting, with means that make radio signals seem like two cups on a string, extinction in appearance only.

In our hypothetical "what-if" of humanity's future, could a blend of technology and greater understanding of the universe help us climb the ladder to an unfamiliar place only glimpsed by spirituality and science alike? Beyond preconceptions, it's feasible we will have staked our claim first to the observable sky.

Befuddled with their findings, our travelers elect to travel back and take smaller jumps ahead to establish a timeline of events. Their fictional account might read something like this:

We've traveled to the year 2070, only to find the world has been through some massive cataclysm. Speaking to several individuals in a nearby Canadian settlement, we learned the unthinkable had happened. There had been a limited nuclear war, madness resulting from a split-second misunderstanding, exactly the sort of scenario the scientific community had warned us about. The politicians and presiding military bodies had turned it off as quickly as it had started, but devastation resulted nonetheless. The many regions not targeted militarily still were forced to contend with a collapsed world economy. In the decades following, nations had reestablished contact. The few billion inhabitants remaining were collectively determined on reformation in the form of a shared philosophy of global betterment as a political and social imperative. It seemed a new age of enlightenment was upon us, though the price had been almost too great to bear. Near-extinction had made an excellent persuader.

In the year 2270, we found a great ring stretched across the southern sky in a slightly paler shade of blue, reflected sunlight from

*outside the atmosphere. It also seemed odd that nearby settlements
had since been abandoned and reclaimed by foliage. Our team
traced a radio signal to a location several thousand kilometers
away, in the region previously known as the nation of Ecuador. We
took the journey, eager to find the source. Then stowing our craft
away in stealth configuration, we made the last kilometer on foot
and encountered a group of researchers taking soil samples. They
appeared puzzled that we were there, but listened to our cover story
with mild interest. We explained that we, too, were researchers, from
another part of the world. It's not clear if they believed this, or
simply humored us, but they nonetheless treated us with kindness
and professionalism. As dusk fell, we accompanied them up to
the ring by way of space elevator.* The hub straddling the carbon
nanotube trunks that stretched into the sky made the thirty-hour
journey to geosynchronous orbit surprisingly pleasant and efficient.
Encircling the Earth, the ring itself was a biosphere lush with
vegetation, mimicking the surface, while hundreds of large modules
slowly spun to simulate gravity. Every human child possessed the
opportunity to gaze down upon the Earth from many thousands of
kilometers up as a part of everyday life. A great rail transportation
system ran through the unimaginable length of the ring, connecting
every portion of it to every other. It was undoubtedly humanity's
greatest achievement. After some investigation, we learned that
nearly all of the population had relocated there out of a collective
sense of obligation, after having devastated the ecosystem. Earth*

---

* Like a ball on a string, a payload at the end of a sturdy enough cable would
remain in orbit, allowing for the easy transport of materials into space.

itself had become a protected zone, save research outposts and science expeditions, explaining the reaction we initially received.

Jumping ahead to the year 2470, we were shocked to find the ring had disappeared. After several hours of theorizing what could have transpired, a solitary figure appeared to our team, seemingly out of thin air. Strangely, this unusually tall woman knew who we were, and the nature of our mission, addressing us each by name. She informed us we were not allowed to stay for any length of time, but politely agreed to answer our questions before our return to our own era. It seemed humanity had been busy in the last couple of centuries, experimenting with interstellar travel, opening pocket universes, and attaining sturdier, even less corporeal forms. AI civilization had fully integrated with our own, a revelation to which our team members had mixed reactions. Intertwined at the deepest levels with our technological progeny, human beings attained metaphysical levels of activity not previously available, effectively becoming extinct as purely biological creatures. She went on to explain that what she called "Metahumanity" had removed the ring from Earth's skies, replacing it with an undetectable exotic matter equivalent to an observation platform to observe the development below. As she spoke, the realization slowly dawned that we had found a world untouched by civilization several centuries in the future because our distant descendants had deliberately removed all signs of human habitation, creating a clean slate for more intelligent biological species to develop. Humanity had left the home that gave us life, in stages, as it evolved. It wasn't until later that it was discovered that the tall woman I had encountered actually appeared as a different figure for each member of the team, and unbeknownst to the group at the time, spoke to each of us in our native language.

It is a tale woven in the spirit of science fiction. There certainly need not be a cataclysm for us to reach our greatest potential. In fact, it stands to reason such an event would probably have the opposite effect, plunging the world into darkness before our irrevocable extinction. There are many paths the future might take, but we can rely on two certainties: that harnessing humanity's best potential will be contingent on continuing down the road of intellectual exploration, and that the world that results will be vastly different from the world we know today.

Gloria is the embodiment of humanity. She speaks for us in her trepidation of straying too far from the comfort zone of the cave at dusk, but also in her daring in venturing to the mouth of the cave to witness the first stars appear. Where we come from, where we are going, it is possible the answers to these questions are one and the same. It is we, the universe, in human form. What we are, have been, or ever will be is the primal made into complexity, as natural as any star, or comet, or moon. We fashion a trail through unknowns and assumptions with reason, critical thinking, and logic hand-in-hand with the creative faith that only imagination can provide. It takes both, and both apparent extremes take us to a larger context. We've known this place all along. Only the descriptions change. And this mezzanine from which we could see the universe from a higher vantage point, that vantage point lies within us, in our willingness to question our preconceptions and establish our priorities as a species.

Gloria intuitively knows she is a projection of the universe, the same as any bubbling brook, leaf caught on the breeze, or the points of light in the sky that follow the setting sun. Intuitively, she knows there are far more expressions she cannot yet know, the language of the spirits made practical. Brushing off her savagery, and putting on her best face, someday soon she might trudge up the long trail of inquiry to meet them.

Before germ theory, disease was allegedly caused by "humors," or the "play of cosmic light and shadow."* [52] A handful of physicians tried to debunk these ideas with radical speculation, and were scoffed at and discredited as a result. They proposed that disease was caused by particulates *too small to see*. Hungarian doctor Ignaz Semmelweis spearheaded the effort to promote handwashing, making the connection that diseases were being carried on doctors' hands from dissections to new mothers in the hospital's maternity ward. For his efforts, his contemporaries saw to it his reputation was ruined, and he didn't live long enough to see his innovation become standard practice. [53]

When one opens a car door, literally millions of bacteria are killed in microseconds as differences in air pressure expel them out into a foreign, often hostile environment. [54] These tiny, yet

---

* It should be noted that at the time, scientific methodology was still being tweaked.

complex molecular machines are not dissimilar from the materials and processes that comprise us at very small scales. An animal cell is arguably as complex as a bustling city. We can imagine being in this tiny realm with molecules that fit together in different configurations of life. The slender, phospholipid molecules composing the cell membrane behave like a tightly packed crowd in a tiny amphitheater, some switching places with the concertgoer next to them millions of times a second, resulting in an ever-dynamic mosaic. A stunning *500 quadrillion* chemical reactions take place in the human body every second. There are no trials and tribulations here. Death and despair, these are perceptions in the macroworld. We are scarcely aware of this undulating ocean of activity that pulses on those microscopic levels. It is difficult to imagine such a tumultuous world reshaping itself time and again far more quickly than we can form a single thought. By the same token, one of your cells could scarcely imagine the range or scale of physical and mental activity available to you.

Again, our sense of scale impedes us in our reasoning. Aristotle, a leading mind in Ancient Greece, reasoned that the stars could not be suns, for this would make them impossibly far away. At the time, it was believed that the stars of the heavens jeweled one of several celestial spheres surrounding the earth. Because this model could not account for the retrograde motion of the planets, scholars of the era surmised that the planets had their own turning spheres, or epicycles. This still didn't quite match the movements of the heavens, but was nevertheless maintained for nearly twenty centuries.

Initial assumptions operate even when we aren't sure where they came from. Sometimes the premise we start out with is wrong, and it takes courage to reexamine what we thought was true. There were no crystal spheres, it turned out. And there were two fatal flaws with the model. For one, the Earth was not at the center. In fact, in the larger scheme it was fairly incidental. The second flaw began with an insistence on circular orbits exemplifying divine perfection. Even today, this determined desire to find divinity in the observable world and the heavens stubbornly persists, a predisposition rooted in magical thinking.

Clarity often begins by seeking out a more viable context. This is the rationality behind the generalized spiritual framework. The equal grounds premise consists of this simplistic model based on scales of consciousness *as a hypothetical,* one which can never be dismissed entirely, paired with what we know for sure of the physical world, based on our predictable experience within it. It constitutes a bridge beneath an enormous sky, the unknown possibilities regarding our existence, individually, and en masse. The universe is a big place. It could be bigger in ways we cannot account for, analogous to the way in which a single cell is incapable of understanding the extraordinary dimensions of comprehension and activities of the larger organism of which it is a part. The nonbeliever asks for proof of a mystical realm so far outside the domain of objective evidence. The mental language of science hasn't the terms to easily describe such a context, where mathematics is replaced by an emotional connection to an invisible world. Addressing the query with one of his or her own, the spiritualist requires proof that the information picture *doesn't* continue far beyond our present circle of knowledge, even so far as underpinning our own existence in a deeply personal way. It's a glass half-full, half-empty proposition, depending on the initial assumption one operates under.

But let's be real, we are not automatons devoted to pure logic, nor can we truly make ourselves believe something that needs constant reinforcement. Each of us has *some* degree of pragmatic skepticism and *some* degree of fanciful thinking, whether we like it or not. What we are really talking about is being comfortable with ambiguity, from *either* side of the fence, when it applies. Perhaps we don't have to choose, but simply practice a measure of self-honesty, giving credit where it is due while striving to understand the thinking behind all philosophical positions. In this light, the equal grounds premise could be thought of as embracing knowledge and doubt alike, while postulating the possibilities of what lies beyond life. The degree of acceptance of the latter part relies on the individual's propensity for spirituality, and would vary from person to person.

Again, science itself cannot change its methodology, but personal attitudes can change. We can experience love. We find joy in activities that make life worthwhile. These emotional states can be relegated to neurotransmitters in the brain, but what of the view of the poet, the artist, who would surely speak to another component? Even to the reductionist mind, there is an ineffable substance to these abstract states that give them value. One can find beauty in an impressionist painting on a gallery wall, or a photo portraying a sea of galaxies framing potentially quadrillions of different sunsets on Earth-like worlds. Appreciation in all its forms is a language of its own. If we have souls, then we also exist outside ourselves in an expansive sky of bright possibilities. If we do not have souls, we need not speculate far past the depths of the heart, for that appreciation for beauty, knowledge, and goodness is something nested within that each of us could call our own.

NOTES

Introduction

1   Carl Sagan, *Cosmos* (New York: Ballantine Books, a division of Random House, Inc., 1980).

2   Jane Roberts, *Seth Speaks: The Eternal Validity of the Soul,* ed. Robert Butts (San Rafael: Amber-Allen Publishing; New World Library, [1972] 1994).

Chapter One

3   Carl Sagan, *Cosmos* (New York: Ballantine Books, a division of Random House, Inc., 1980), 105.

4   Ibid., 140.

5   Jenkins, Daniel G, "Reason, Knowledge, and Belief." Reading class lecture, PHIL143: Introduction to the Study of Religion from Montgomery College, Silver Spring, MD, June 16, 2019.

Chapter Two

6   Mark Leary, *Understanding the Mysteries of Human Behavior* (Chantilly, VA: The Teaching Company, 2012), 123.

7   Mark Leary, *Understanding the Mysteries of Human Behavior* (2012; Chantilly, VA: The Teaching Company, 2012), DVD.

8   Mark Leary, *Understanding the Mysteries of Human Behavior* (Chantilly, VA: The Teaching Company, 2012), 125.

9   Ibid., 126.

10 Max Planck. AZQuotes.com, Wind and Fly LTD, 2019, accessed November 26, 2019, https://www.azquotes.com/quote/1055635.

11 Dan Jones, "Free will persists (even if your brain made you do it)," *New Scientist,* September 19, 2014, accessed November

20, 2019, https://www.newscientist.com/article/dn26242-free-will-persists-even-if-your-brain-made-you-do-it/.

Chapter Three

12 René Descartes, *Meditations and Other Metaphysical Writings*, trans. Desmond M. Clarke (New York: Penguin Putnam, Inc., 1998), 18-70.

13 Erica Carlson, *Understanding the Quantum World* (2019; Chantilly, VA: The Teaching Company, 2019), DVD.

14 Erica Carlson, *Understanding the Quantum World* (Chantilly, VA: The Teaching Company, 2019), 31.

15 Carl Jung. AZQuotes.com, Wind and Fly LTD, 2019, accessed November 26, 2019, https://www.azquotes.com/quote/355847.

16 Michael Talbot, *The Holographic Universe* (New York: Harper Collins Publishers, 1991), 191-192.

17 Seth Schwartz, "Do We Have Free Will?: Is free choice real, or is it just an illusion?," *Psychology Today*, Nov 19, 2013, accessed November 20, 2019, https://www.psychologytoday.com/us/blog/proceed-your-own-risk/201311/do-we-have-free-will.

Chapter Four

18 Michael Talbot, *The Holographic Universe* (New York: Harper Collins Publishers, 1991), 46-48.

19 Niels Bohr. AZQuotes.com, Wind and Fly LTD, 2019, accessed November 26, 2019, https://www.azquotes.com/quote/30770.

Chapter Five

20 "Rebooting the Cosmos: Is the Universe the Ultimate Computer?," online video, 1:31:12, posted by World Science Festival, 2011, https://www.worldsciencefestival.com/videos/rebooting-the-cosmos-is-the-universe-the-ultimate-computer/.

21 Tom Campbell, "My Interview with Tom Campbell," interview by Chris Delamo, Red Pill Philosophy, 1:43:48, October

18, 2013, http://redpill.boards.net/thread/7/interview-tom-campbell-video.

22 Norman Friedman, *Bridging Science and Spirit: Common Elements In David Bohm's Physics, The Perennial Philosophy and Seth* (The Woodbridge Group, 1993), 142.

23 Shana Kelley and Ted Sargent, *Introduction to Nanotechnology: The New Science of Small* (Chantilly, VA: The Teaching Company, 2012), 25-26.

Chapter Six

24 Anita Moorjani, *Dying to be Me: My Journey From Cancer, to Near Death, to True Healing* (Hay House, Inc., 2012), 71.

25 Ibid., 71-72.

26 Michael Talbot, *The Holographic Universe* (New York: Harper Collins Publishers, 1991), 240.

27 Ibid., 242.

28 Ibid., 241-242.

29 P.M.H Atwater, "Unpleasant and/or Hell-like Experience," in *Beyond the Light: What Isn't Being Said About Near Death Experiences,* rev. ed. (Kill Devil Hills, NC: Transpersonal Publishing, div. AHU, LLC, [1994] 2009), 27-45.

30 Raymond Moody Jr., *Life After Life* (New York: Bantam Books, [1975] 1976. Published by arrangement with Mockingbird Books.), 28-34, 58-73.

31 Tim Newman, "Near-death experiences: Fact or fantasy?" *Medical News Today,* April 27, 2016, accessed January 15, 2020, https://www.medicalnewstoday.com/articles/309454.php#11.

32 Ian Stevenson, *Children Who Remember Previous Lives: A Question of Reincarnation,* rev. ed. (Jefferson, NC: McFarland & Company, Inc., [1987] 2001).

33 Ibid., 29.

34 Ibid., 38.

35 Jane Roberts, "Reincarnational Dramas," in *Seth Speaks: The Eternal Validity of the Soul*, ed. Robert Butts (San Rafael: Amber-Allen Publishing; New World Library, [1972] 1994), 46-59.

Chapter Seven

36 Jane Roberts, *The Nature of Personal Reality: Specific, Practical Techniques for Solving Everyday Problems and Enriching the Life You Know* (San Rafael: Amber-Allen Publishing; New World Library, [1974] 1994), 14.

37 Jane Roberts, *The Individual and the Nature of Mass Events* (San Rafael: Amber-Allen Publishing, [1981] 1995), 31.

38 Jane Roberts, *Seth Speaks: The Eternal Validity of the Soul*, ed. Robert Butts (San Rafael: Amber-Allen Publishing; New World Library, [1972] 1994), 49-52.

39 Ibid., 222-224.

40 Jane Roberts, *Dreams, "Evolution," and Value Fulfillment*, vol. 2 (San Rafael: Amber-Allen Publishing, [1986] 1995), 341.

41 Jane Roberts, *Seth Speaks: The Eternal Validity of the Soul*, ed. Robert Butts (San Rafael: Amber-Allen Publishing; New World Library, [1972] 1997), 328-329.

42 Jane Roberts, *The Nature of Personal Reality: Specific, Practical Techniques for Solving Everyday Problems and Enriching the Life You Know* (San Rafael: Amber-Allen Publishing; New World Library, [1974] 1994), 16-17.

Chapter Eight

43 Carl Sagan, BrainyQuote.com, BrainyMedia Inc., 2019, accessed November 26, 2019, https://www.brainyquote.com/quotes/carl_sagan_130525.

44 Carl Sagan, BrainyQuote.com, BrainyMedia Inc., 2020, accessed January 10, 2020, https://www.brainyquote.com/quotes/carl_sagan_124576.

45 Carl Sagan, Goodreads, Inc., 2020, accessed January 3, 2020, https://www.goodreads.com/quotes/8385-in-science-it-often-happens-that-scientists-say-you-know.

46 Carl Sagan, *Cosmos* (New York: Ballantine Books, a division of Random House, Inc., 1980), 10-12, 276-279.

47 Gabriel Rotello, *Doomsday: 10 Ways the World Will End, Solar Storm*, directed by Gabriel Rotello (2016; New York, NY: History Channel, 2016), video.

Chapter Nine

48 Amy Gunia, "The Navy Is Working on Guidelines for Reporting UFOs After Pilots Pushed to Have Sightings Taken Seriously," *Time*, April 25, 2019, accessed January 31, 2020, https://time.com/5577853/navy-ufo-reporting-guidelines/.

49 Arthur C. Clarke, *2001: A Space Odyssey* (New York: ROC, [1968] 1993).

50 Arthur C. Clarke and Frederik Pohl, *The Last Theorem* (New York: Ballantine Books; DelRey, 2008).

51 Arthur C. Clarke and Stephen Baxter, *Time's Eye* (New York: Ballantine, 2004).

52 Bruce Fleury, *Mysteries of the Microscopic World* (2011; Chantilly, VA: The Teaching Company, 2011), DVD.

53 Bruce Fleury, *Mysteries of the Microscopic World* (Chantilly, VA: The Teaching Company, 2012), 16.

54 Bruce Fleury, *Mysteries of the Microscopic World* (2012; Chantilly, VA: The Teaching Company, 2012), DVD.

Lightning Source UK Ltd.
Milton Keynes UK
UKHW010629010321
379583UK00001B/80